SEWING

Create Your Own Beautiful and Safe Sewing
Items and Easy Sewing Projects

(Learn to Sew Quickly and Easily With This
Step-by-step Guide for Beginners)

Lawrence Smith

Published By **Lawrence Smith**

Lawrence Smith

All Rights Reserved

Sewing: Create Your Own Beautiful and Safe Sewing Items and Easy Sewing Projects (Learn to Sew Quickly and Easily With This Step-by-step Guide for Beginners)

ISBN 978-1-77485-428-0

All rights reserved. No part of this guide may be reproduced in any form without permission in writing from the publisher except in the case of brief quotations embodied in critical articles or reviews.

Legal & Disclaimer

The information contained in this book is not designed to replace or take the place of any form of medicine or professional medical advice. The information in this book has been provided for educational and entertainment purposes only.

The information contained in this book has been compiled from sources deemed reliable, and it is accurate to the best of the Author's knowledge; however, the Author cannot guarantee its accuracy and validity and cannot be held liable for any errors or omissions. Changes are periodically made to this book. You must consult your doctor or get professional medical advice before using any of the suggested remedies, techniques, or information in this book.

Upon using the information contained in this book, you agree to hold harmless the Author from and against any damages, costs, and expenses, including any legal fees potentially resulting from the application of any of the information provided by this guide. This disclaimer applies to any damages or injury caused by the use and application, whether directly or indirectly, of any advice or information presented, whether for breach of contract, tort, negligence, personal injury, criminal intent, or under any other cause of action.

You agree to accept all risks of using the information presented inside this book. You need to consult a professional medical practitioner in order to ensure you are both able and healthy enough to participate in this program.

TABLE OF CONTENTS

INTRODUCTION 1

CHAPTER 1: SEWING BASICS 3

CHAPTER 2: NEEDLE AND THREAD TIPS 14

CHAPTER 3: THE BASIC STITCHES 21

CHAPTER 4: ACCURATE MEASUREMENTS 36

CHAPTER 5: A SIMPLE PILLOW BAGS, BAGS, AND HOME DECOR PROJECTS 45

CHAPTER 6: EASY CLOTHING PROJECTS 58

CHAPTER 7: WHERE TO BEGIN 68

CHAPTER 8: TOOLS REQUIRED TO QUILT 74

CHAPTER 9: EVERYTHING ABOUT QUILT BLOCKS 83

CHAPTER 10: MAKING YOUR FIRST QUILT: STEP BY STEP GUIDE 90

CHAPTER 11: CONNECTING THE BACK OF THE QUILT 97

CHAPTER 12: PROPER EDGING 100

CHAPTER 13: WHY YOU SHOULD LEARN SEWING 103

CHAPTER 14: EQUIPMENT AND DEVICES NEEDED FOR SEWING 108

CHAPTER 15: SEWING MACHINE AND ITS BASICS 118

CHAPTER 16: THE FUNDAMENTAL SEWING TECHNIQUES 128

CHAPTER 17: THE SPECIAL TECHNIQUES FOR SEWING... 140

CHAPTER 18: SEWING TUTORIALS- SIMPLE TO FOLLOW 152

CHAPTER 19: MAKING SEWING PATTERNS FOR BEGINNERS 165

CHAPTER 20: SEWING TIPS TO HELP BEGIN 173

CHAPTER 21: ADVANCED SEWING TECHNIQUES YOU SHOULD BE EDUCATED.. 178

CONCLUSION.. 183

Introduction

Sewing is among the old-fashioned hobbies that lots of people have enjoyed in the past. However, this doesn't mean that you shouldn't be able to appreciate it in the present.

In reality, sewing is among the most beneficial things that you can learn. It is not just an enjoyable way of passing your time, but it will teach you the skills you'll need to sew buttons, fix hemlinesand buttons, alter the design, and make projects that leave you and your friends and family members in stupor!

This book is packed with practical steps and techniques which will make your aim of learning to sew easy and doable. Beginning with basic techniques and tools through to practical or wearable designs, it has all the necessary information to improve your sewing skills to their maximum potential.

What are you waiting on?

Go through this book and become a skilled sewist in just a few minutes!

thank you for download this Book. I hope you like it!

Chapter 1: Sewing Basics

Before you begin sewing, you must be sure that you have the correct equipment.

Sewing Needles

The first step is to be equipped with sewing notions. They include:

* Thread. It's best to invest in the right thread at the start. It is important to have several kinds and colors to pick from when you are working on your projects. While it might be tempting to purchase inexpensive thread in bulk however, you

should ensure the thread you choose is of high-quality. Threads that aren't of the highest quality break, fray and tear easily, and can result in irritation. Gutterman along with Coats and Clark are good brands to start with.

* Needle Threader. A needle threader has the thin wire loop which helps you thread even the most tiny needles. They're a cheap purchase that is useful for both hand - and machine-sewing projects.

• Hand sewing needles. Hand sewing needles are available in a variety of sizes and point styles , which are suitable for different kinds of stitches.

* Sewing Machine Needles. These needles are specifically designed specifically for sewing machines, and all project you can make using them. When you are machines, you need to begin each project by using a different needle. In the beginning, you should select needles that fall in the categories of 80/12 or 75/11 which is also known as Universal Needles. Select 70/10 if you're working on thin and

lightweight fabric. Learn more about this within the following chapter.

* Pins/Pincushion. The best pins have colored balls on top and are also known as straight steel pins. They are simple to grab and put in. Also, make sure you have a pincushion on hand so that you don't leave the pins scattered around. It is also possible to make use of magnetic dishes as pin holders if you wish.

* Thimbles. If you're sensitive to pain when it is even the smallest form of pain, then you could purchase thimbles to prevent your thumbs safe from being pinched.

In addition to sewing notions There are other sewing tools will be required. See them below.

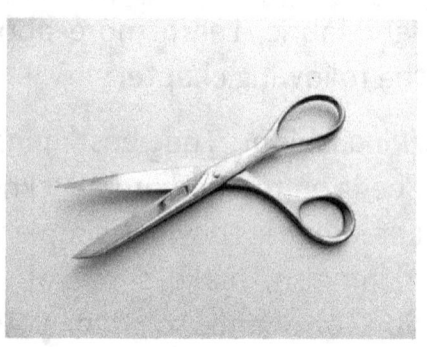

Cutting Tools

Naturally, you'll also require tools to cut your thread as well as fabrics to make the pieces you create. Being sharp and precise when cutting is vital for sewing. these tools can help you accomplish that and more!

* Shears. Shears can be useful since you'll be cutting lots of fabric, and your basic pair of scissors can't handle fabric.

* Scissors. Scissors with bent edges can be helpful for cutting threads and fabric that is light as well as being more convenient than shears.

* Rotary Cutter. Rotary cutters help cut thread and fabric exactly the way you

desire, and aid in creating straight edges. They are best employed for cutting long pieces and curves.

* Seam Ripper. Seam rippers are a cost-effective device that comes in handy when you have to rectify your mistakes. The name implies that when you notice seams when you're working it is possible to fix the seams using this.

Marking Tools

The importance of marking your projects is crucial because it lets you identify the best places to cut, pin and sew.

* Fabric Pencils. Contrary to standard pencils, fabric pencils are made of special lead that lets them be visible even on the darkest of fabrics. They may also have special erasers or brushes that allow you to erase the marks on your fabric after they're not required anymore.

* Sharpener. Of course, you'll require sharpeners to ensure that your pencils remain sharp, both literally and metaphorically. A standard pencil sharpener is sufficient.

* Fabric Pens. Water-soluble pens can aid in marking fabrics. Marks can be easily removed using an aqueous cloth.

* Fabric Chalk. Fabric chalk, also known as tailor's chalk is another alternative. Although white chalk may be utilized, it's not necessarily the best option due to the fact that chalk marks can get smudged and peel off easily.

Measuring Instruments

Measurements of your fabric are essential. It is important to measure accurately. This will protect you from the frustration when you finish a project finding it to be too big, too small or is not correctly formed. Making accurate measurements will prevent you time spent making corrections, and will help you create the best quality finished product. Let's talk about the equipment you'll require.

* Ruler. A 6 ' long, clear ruler can give you precise measurements. It will also allow you to cut clean, straight cuts using the circular cutter.

* Seam Gauge. It is tiny ruler employed for small tasks such as marking seams and creating seam allowances.

* Tape Measure. Tape measures can be useful to align patterns and measuring long fabrics as well as three-dimensional objects. Use flexible tapes that are able to adapt to different dimensions and shapes.

• Long metal rulers/T-squares. These aren't needed often except for when working on large and lengthy projects. However, it's best to get some and keep them around in case you need them.

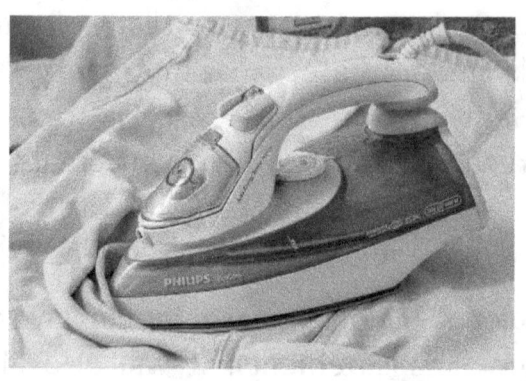

Pressing Tools

Of course for making your work easier to present and cleaner it is also necessary to be equipped with some tools for pressing.

* Ironing Board. A standard size is sufficient, but bear in mind that they come in different sizes too. Apart from being helpful to your projects it is also a great way to make use of it in your daily routine, as well!

* Steam Iron. Select a trusted manufacturer of steam irons that is heated evenly and can be adjusted to different steam settings to meet the variety of fabrics you could use.

* Mini Iron. This is intended to be used for lighter and smaller sizes of fabric that don't have the capacity to take on too much heat.

*Pressing Cloths. Pressing cloths will stop unnecessary heat, especially on delicate fabrics or cloths and protects the quality of your designs.

The Pressing Hams. Pressing hams makes ironing difficult to reach edges and bends seams and hems more easily.

* Folding Pen. With folding pens, it is easy to make precise folds in fabric. They also help keep the folds neat and well-placed to ensure that you don't burn your fingers trying to keep the hem in position while ironing.

Basic Sewing Machines

If you're planning on using an sewing machine for your work It's best to ensure that it's the best one in your possession.

The sewing machines listed here will accomplish the task.

* Blue Tip/Singer/Q Needle. This is a stretch needle point and is best employed to avoid stitch skips and snagging. This is also best for knits and microfibers as well as other materials.

* European 130/705HJ. This machine uses the Tightly Woven Fabric system , and is best for denim, upholstery and the largest kinds of corduroys.

* American 15 1DE. These needles are sharp and are best employed for sewing jeans or denim as well as other heavy fabric.

*130/705H, or 15 1DE American. This is perfect for those who are just beginning, as it is an all-purpose sewing machine that is compatible with all kinds of threads and fabrics.

Chapter 2: Needle And Thread Tips

Thread and needles are among the most essential sewing supplies that you require. In this article you'll find out more about them as well as how to make sure your have only the best one in your arsenal.

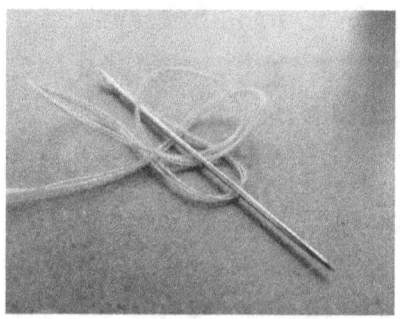

Needles

The best size to use is 75/11 (American) or 80/12 (European)

Keep in mind that anything larger than 80 is considered to be a large needle. You can utilize the smaller 60/8 needle for sewing delicate fabrics, such as light curtains or clothes. Needles made in the 120/19 range meet the requirements of more heavy fabrics and projects without breaking and generally are the best choice for home décor projects.

Parts of the Needle

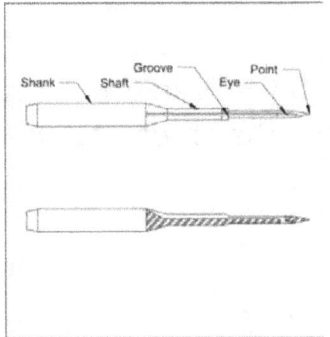

* Shaft. This is the term used to describe the body of the needle. Be aware the different types of needles come with different sizes.

* Shank. This is the portion of the needle which is connected to the machine, when you're using one.

* Eye. This is the place where you'll thread the thread and is the most well recognized component of needles.

* Scarf. Do you see that tiny line near the eye? This is referred to as the scarf. If you're using bobbincase hooks, this comes in handy as it will keep the bobbins near to the eye , so it is possible to make a stitch and hold it in place.

* Front Groove. The front groove as a direction for the thread as it passes into the eyes of the needle.

Heavy Duty Needles

Here are some more powerful needles that are ideal for large-duty tasks.

* Metallic. They are best for topstitching and embellishments and are specifically designed to be used with metallic threads as well as other specialty threads that are susceptible to breaking and shredding. The metallic needle has an eye that is larger for easy threading.

* Sharps. The needles mentioned above are best employed for microfibers and silk since they are sharper.

* Leather. This is best utilized for genuine leather since it comes with an chisel-point at the top.

* Jeans. This sturdy, sharp needle is designed for handling denim, canvas as well as other heavy and tightly-woven materials .

Threads

The next step is a quick and easy guide to threads!

Thread Types

* Cotton. Cotton is the most widely used kind of thread and is best employed for delicately weaved or medium to light textiles with little or no stretch. Always opt for 100 percent cotton thread.

* 100% Egyptian. This premium thread, with a high-gloss finish, is ideal for machine sewing and hand sewing. This is the kind of thread that is used to make 1600 - 1800 thread count blankets and pillows and is also used to quilt natural fibers.

* Polyester. A different type of thread is polyester, which you will find in a lot of shops for sewing and embroidery. Polyester thread is durable and durable and is suitable for virtually any kind of fabrics, and also for interior decor. It is suitable in both machine and hand sewing and is ideal for stretch, permanent press or knit fabric due to its resistance and ability to recover. Choose XP Plus Polyester if you're looking for a stronger version.

* Rayon/Trilobal Polyester. These threads are designed to be used for machine sewing since they're made for hassle-free sewing with a smooth , smooth finish. They are also a popular choice in the market and can be used with all types of embroidery. Although it's slightly more costly, trilobal polyester is superior to rayon due to its strength and colorfastness.

* Silk. Silk is an extremely elastic thread that is able to work with even the most delicate kinds of fabrics. It's sturdy, and best employed for hand-tacking as well as securing hems and hand basting. Silk thread is also less likely to get caught than other threads. This makes hand sewing much simpler.

* Metallic. Metallic thread is made of metallic strands of thread that are wrapped around polyester cores. It is used in conjunction with metal needles, and it is best employed for decoration or for home decor.

* Others. Other threads include beading, nylon, upholstery, pre-wound, bobbins, microfilament and wool. There are also glow-in the dark threads which can be utilized for specific projects.

Chapter 3: The Basic Stitches

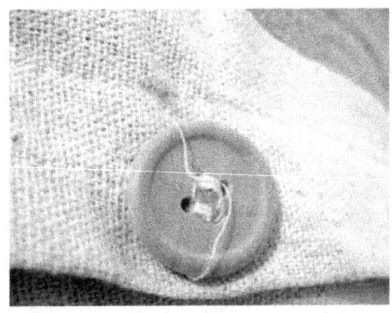

Now that you've identified what you should have in your kit now is the time to master the fundamental stitches!

1. Sewing Seams

The first thing to be aware of when working on seams is that you are able to utilize thread in two methods: Double or Single threading. Here's how:

• Single threading. After you've inserted it into your eye take it out, making sure that it's just two inches from the other end of your needle. Cut the thread to the length you prefer tie it up, then begin sewing.

Double Threading. Thread the thread into an eye on the needle and then increase it to ensure that you obtain a more robust type of thread. Let the ends of the thread connect with the thread that you spooled to create 2 tails. Join these two ends before sewing your fabric with your doubled thread.

Three knots you can tie when trying to stitch seams. You may not need to make them all at the same time. Refer to the following guide for further details.

The First Knot. If you've utilized double threading, be sure you cut the thread is visible below the eye of the needle to create a an ordinary knot with two tails.

2. Second Knot. It can be used to perform double and single threading. First, you must hold the thread with one hand while holding it in another. Then you pull the thread, looping it in a counterclockwise direction to create the beginning of knot. When you transfer the thread onto the fabric, ensure that you tighten it . You can

ensure that the knot is held with just one or more fingers.

The Third Knot. To make this knot you have to stitch a few stitches on the opposite edge of your cloth. Make a loop by slipping the needle through the stitch, then pulling to tighten the knot. Repeat this process twice for the knot to be secured, and you're done.

After you've tied the knot, it's now time to begin stitching. In the beginning, we'll examine two common stitches that are the basting stitch and the running stitch. Make sure that you thread the needle in order to create knot prior to starting.

* Basting Stitch. It is an open temporary stitch that is used to hold each layer of fabric as you sew. It is easily removed using a seam ripper after you've finished. To make your basting stitch you need to make approximately 1/8 " or 1/4 " long stitches according to the length you'd like to sew.

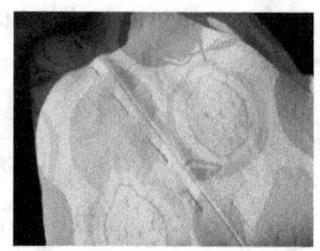

* Run Stitch. It is an easy stitch that is commonly used for sewing. It's similar in design with the basting stitches however, the stitches are positioned closer to each other since they are meant to last. Begin stitching from the point the point you first insert the thread. Then, stitch across the entire long length that you are stitching by passing the needle into then out. Continue to keep "running" till you have to.

Backstitching

Nowis the time to back stitch. Backstitching is a simple and durable stitch that can make your creations appear as they were completed using machines.

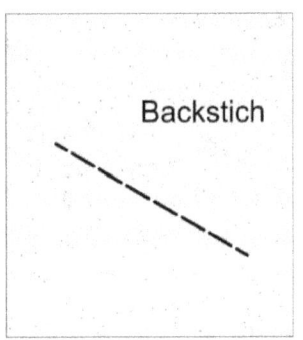

Backstich

To reverse stitch, start by threading your needle , then tie the ends of your thread. Insert the needle on an opposite side, then pull until you get to the knot you made earlier.

Begin making small stitches starting around the knot to either the either the left or right. Once you've reached your starting point on the opposite part of the fabric in the position that is one stitch more wide than the one before. Keep in mind that it's the responsibility of you to make sure that the stitches are at the same distance or as wide as you can. The spacing will always be determined by you, so take into consideration the spacing you'd like to achieve.

Slipstitching

Slipstitching is more complex however, you can easily master it with some practice. Slipstitching lets you create stitches that appear invisible, ensuring that your creations appear flawless.

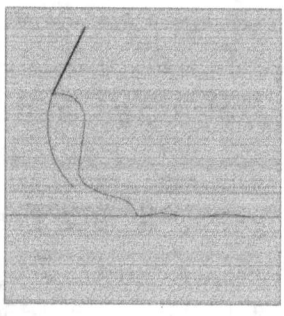

To make slip stitches make a small cut of fabric and push it into the fold after folding in half. Unfold the cloth, and then fold it in such a way that both sides are in the same direction to form toward the middle line. Fold it over the center line, then double threading your needle by inserting the thread into your needle's eye. then double it to create more of a stronger thread. Let the other end of the thread join with the thread that you spooled, in order to have two ends of the tail. Join these two ends before sewing the fabric using the thread that has been doubled.

Then, tie knots using the needle up on top of your cloth. Be sure you remain close to an edge on the folded fabric. Continue pulling until you have caught the knot, then pull it to the last fold of the cloth on the bottom. Insert the needle into the folded part of the cloth. Pull it until you can see around 1/4 inch and then pull it to pull it back. Continue pushing horizontally and repeat the process to the finish.

When you are at the endof your project, you can begin to make tiny stitches on that long folded edge of your cloth. Make sure you pull the thread till you've got one small loop and then insert the needle again. Create an elongated knot through pulling it, and repeat this process until you can fully make it tighter.

Stitches with Decorative Designs

Stitch designs are attractive stitches that can give your project an extra appeal.

* Whip Stitch. To whip stitch make sure you fold the cloth in half, then secure it with a pin to stop it from moving. Put the needle into the top of the fold after opening it. Make sure the needle goes through the back towards the front. After that, you'll need to will make the next couple of stitches at the same height as the first two stitches. Then, finish it off by making blanket stitches, which you'll be able to learn more about later.

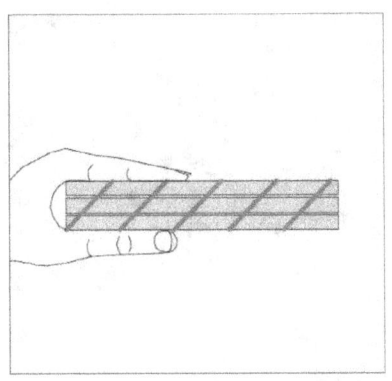

- Blanket Stitch. To create blanket stitches, start at the front of the fabric, and then take the needle away from there. Then thread the needle diagonally , so you can create cross-stitch diagonally across the reverse part of the material. Continue pulling while making diagonal stitches, and finally stop where you will are able to see the biggest type of diagonal stitch.

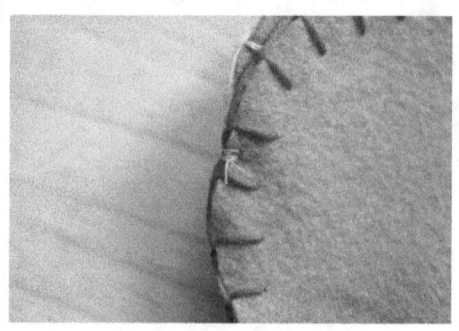

Then, loop the needle across the diagonal, and pull it at an angle of 90 degrees on the stitch. Continue sewing more diagonal stitches. Make sure to sew as many stitches as you need.

To finish the stitch end the stitch, loop the needle over the vertical edge of the fabric. Make another loop. Then , insert the needle at least three times, and then close the stitch by making a knot.

2. French Seams

French seams are going to be extremely beneficial for those who is looking to design your personal home decor, totes purses, bags and other similar items. They can seem a bit difficult at first, but you can figure out how to make them. And you'll discover how in this article!

The most effective method is to create at least 1/8-to 1/4 allowances for seams to avoid cutting off the excess fabric. This will allow your designs to appear more cohesive. Here's a step-by step guide to make it easier for you to understand.

2. Cut 2 pieces of cloth then put them on top of one another making sure that the wrong sides face one another.

Begin from the right side of the fabric, and sew at least 1/8 inches of seam .

* Next you can lay the fabric out and press the seam to ensure that it's flat.

Then, fold the fabric, then start sewing by making sure your right-hand edge remains clearly visible.

* Make sure to use minimum 1/4 inches allowance when sewing. complete the whole width of your seam.

Make use of your iron and press the fabric down starting at the wrong side and working your way until the front. Sewing the seam allowance will result in an even and well-finished project.

3. Sewing Buttons

There are instances when you need sew buttons onto the projects you're working on. This guide will be simple to show you how to sew buttons.

Button Types

There are two types of buttons that you could make use of:

* Shank Buttons. Shank buttons do not have holes the top. However, they do have an open lump at the back, so it is possible to thread them. These buttons are typically worn on dresses and coats.

* Flat Buttons. Flat buttons are those found on the majority of types of clothing, including dresses. They usually contain two to four holes.

What do you require

Here are the things you'll need to sew buttons:

* Buttons

8.8 inches of thread that have been doubled

* Fabric marking pen or pencil

* Needle

How do I do it?

* When making a shank button, mark the location that you'd like to sew the button. The needle you thread to the location you've identified, then slide by the loop that is on both sides of your button.

• Pull thread until that the button rests comfortably against the fabric

* Secure the button on the shank through the thread of the needle through the fabric and down the button's back 8-10 times.

* Next, tie it on the opposite side of the fabric several times to secure the button. Then, cut off the thread that is left.

* If you sew an open button, ensure that you place the button that you would like the button to go.

* Next, loop your needle around the edge of the fabric close to the point you drawn.

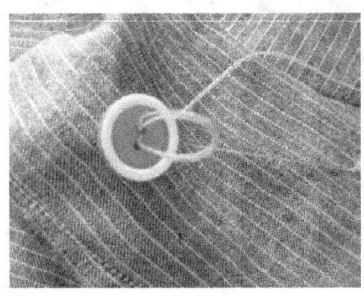

* Thread the needle into one of the button holes before reversing it back down through the other hole and into the fabric. The thread should be pulled tight until the button rests against the fabric. Then continue to loop it through hole for it to be secured in the fabric.

It's done! You're all set to go!

Chapter 4: Accurate Measurements

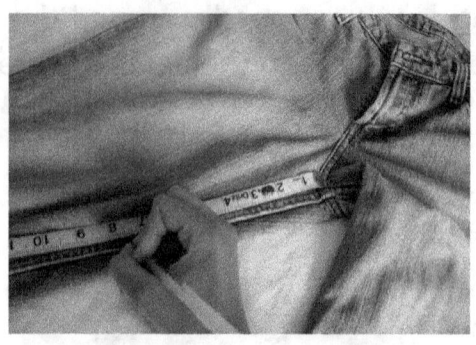

Accurate measurements are crucial when it comes to sewing to ensure that you don't spend time and effort, and of course thread, needles, or fabric. This section will give you an overview of how to measure pillows and garments and how to accurately take measurements of your body for sewing clothes. Take a look at the guidelines below.

Pillow Cover Measurements

Pillow covers are among the most simple and affordable sewing projects you can tackle. Here's a list of different types of pillows along with the measurements they correspond to.

Standard Pillow

Dimensions 20 26 inches

Quantity of Fabric Required: 5/8 Yard

Square Pillows

There are various dimensions to these, and you can read below:

30 x 30 inches - 1 yard

20 x 20 inches - 3/4 yard

18 x 18 inches - 5/8 yard

16 x 16 inches - 1/2 yard

14 x 14 inches - 1/2 yard

12 x 12 inches - 1/3 yard

Queen Size Pillows

Dimensions 20 30 inches x 20 inches

Quantity of Fabric Required 1 and 1/8 yard

King Size Pillows

Dimensions 20 36 inches

Quantity of Fabric Required 1 and 1/8 yard

Measurements for Garments

Measurements for clothing isn't always easy due to the variety of sizes and styles of clothing. It is helpful to have a reference to help you get an idea of approximate measurements that can be used for various body types, such as the one below.

A long sleeved, long-sleeved dress paired

35 to 36 inches 5 yards

44-45 inches 3 and 5/8 miles

50 inches three and 1/4 yards

52-54 inches - 3,1/8 and 52 inches

56 - 60 inches - 3 yards

Straight skirt

35 to 36 inches four and 1/4 yard

44-45 inches 3 , 1/8 yard

50 inches two and 3/4 yards

52-54 inches two and five/8 yard

56 - 60 inches - two and three-quarter yards

Bias Cut Camisole

35-36 inches - 1-1/2 yards

44 to 45 inches 1,3 yards

50 inches 1 and 1/4 yards

52-54 inches - 1-1/8 yards

56 to 60 inches 1 yard

Cap-sleeved Blouse

35 to 36 inches 1-1/2 yards

44 to 45 inches 1-1/2 yards

50 inches 1 and 1/4 yards

52 to 54 inches 1-1/8 yards

56 - 60 inches - 1 yard

Long sleeved blouse tied with a tie

35-36 inches - 3 and 1/4 yards

44 to 45 inches 2,7/8 yard

50 inches 2 and 5/8 yard

52-54 inches - 2,3/8 and 2 yards

56 - 60 inches - two and 1/4 yards

Long sleeved blouse or shirt

35 to 36 inches 2,5 yards

44-45 inches - 2 , 1/8 yard

50 inches 1,3 yards

52 to 54 inches one and 1/4 yards

56 - 60 inches one and five/8 yard

Blouse/short sleeved t-shirt

35-36 inches - 2 yards

44-45 inches 1,5/8 yard

50 inches one and a half yards

52 to 54 inches one and three-quarter yards

56 - 60 inches 1,4 yards

A softly the skirt is gathered

35-36 inches - 2 , 1/4 and 35 inches

44-45 inches - 1-1/2 yards

50 inches 1 and 5/8 yard

52-54 inches - 1-1/2 yards

56 - 60 inches - 1-1/2 yards

A-line skirt

35-36 inches - 2 , 1/4 and 35 inches

44-45 inches - 1,3 yards

50 inches 1 and 5/8 yard

52-54 inches - 1-1/2 yards

56 - 60 inches - 1-1/2 yards

Straight Skirt

35 to 36 inches 2 yards

44-45 inches - 1-1/2 yards

50 inches one and a half yards

52-54 inches - 1,3/8 and 52 inches

56 - 60 inches 1,4 yards

Bermuda Shorts

35 to 36 inches 2,5 yards

44-45 inches - two and one-half yards

50 inches 1 and 7/8 miles

52-54 inches - one and 3/4 yards

56 - 60 inches 1,4 yards

Capri Pants

35-36 inches - two and three quarter yards

44 to 45 inches two and 1/4 yards

50 inches 2 and 1/8 miles

52-54 inches 2 yards

56 to 60 inches 1 , 1/2 yard

Full Length Pants

35-36 inches - 3 , 1/4 and 35 inches

44 to 45 inches 2,5/8 and 44 inches

50 inches 2 and 5/8 yards

52-54 inches - 2 , 1/4 and 52 inches

56-60 inches two and 1/4 yards

How can you get accurate body Measurements

The most important thing is to consider the following measures:

1. Height: Stand barefoot and with your back towards the wall. Start measuring from the floor up from the floor to above your head.

2. Bust: take measurements at the highest point of your chest. Be sure to keep the tape in place and even when wrapping it around your back. The arms should be on your sides as you are taking measurements.

3. Waist: Measure from the waistline (the thinnest portion in the upper torso). Attach a ribbon or string at the natural waistline and hold it in place until the measurement number 5.

4. High bust: place the tape over the bust, then wrap it around the arms, and then straight across the back.

5. Back waist length: take a measurement from the neck's bottom from the base of your neck to where you naturally waist (marked by the string or ribbon).

6. Hips Measurement: wrap the tape around the broadest part of your hips, and at least seven inches lower than the waistline.

Notes:

* Ensure that the body and the floor are parallel when you take measurements of the subject.

Take measurements of the subject when the subject is in only his underwear or wearing a leotard, for more precise measurements.

Don't even try to do your own measurements. This could result in untrue results.

Chapter 5: A Simple Pillow Bags, Bags, And Home Decor Projects

Easy Pillow Cover

What you require:

* A fabric sheet
* Needle
* Thread
* Scissors
* Pillow

Instructions:

It is generally used for pillows with squares, specifically 16x16 sized ones. That means you'll need about 1 yards of material.

Make the cut by adding 2 inches to the width of the opposite side. If your original dimension is 16x16 inches, you'll end up with 16 18 inches wide.

Then, you'll need to take the back from the material, and trim the fabric in half. The right and left edges of the material together , and ensure you are placing on the first piece and sew the opposite side.

* Next, you'll need to take your piece of fabric with the edge that is sewn and join it with the back piece, so that it will overhang what's in front. Keep the fabric in place by pinning them to the floor.

• Sew edges of the fabric together. You can also clip corners if you would like round edges in what you end up with.

After that turn the pillow cover upside down and put your pillow inside.

Enjoy your brand new pillow!

Beautiful Bohemian Pillows

What do you need:

* Needle

* Thread

* Pillow

• One huge sheet of fabric

* Extra fabrics, as appliques

Instructions:

First, gather some remaining fabric, as well as extra fabric you could make appliques from.

Take the pillow you've got and make out a piece of fabric that's at minimum one inch larger than the entire way around.

Now, pin the designs (or apply the spray adhesive).

Make use of the sewing machine to sew the appliques and fabrics down. Running stitches are a good choice for this.

Attach a zipper on the opposite side of the pillow using backstitching and then clipping one side prior to attaching the three sides to the pillow.

* Clip the corners , then press the cover if you wish.

Place the cover over your pillow, and then relax!

Pretty Ribbon Pillowcase

What do you need:

* Different widths and colors of ribbons

* Thread

* Old pillows/pillow forms

* 1/2 yard fleece

Instructions:

Print free patterns on online sites, or create your own pattern then cut the pattern.

* Place your pattern onto the piece of fleece, then pin it down to secure it in the desired position.

* Make use of a running stitch to connect the ribbon to front of the material. You could also use this technique to attach additional ribbons and embellishments, if you'd like.

* Fold the fabric over its back side, about an inch away from the top and then stitch the fabric and appliques by using slip stitches. Only do this if you're not using fleece. Otherwise proceed for the following step.

* Turn the sides of your pillow lie the right way, then lay the pillow flat using pins to keep the pillow secure. Be sure to leave around 1 inch of space to stitch around.

* Flip the right side over and trim corners and any extra threads prior to using it to cover your pillow.

* Add extra ribbons, if desired.

* Enjoy!

Simple and flexible Purse

What do you need:

* Fabric scissors

* Pencil

* Pins

* 1/2 yard solid fabric

* 1/2 yard of patterned fabric

* Thread and needle, to create stitching basting

* Iron

* Thread for machine sewing

Heavy paper or cardstock

* Bag template

Instructions:

* Download a design after having it expanded and printing it on heavy or cardstock. Draw it on both fabrics and cut.

* The two solid pieces join by securing them with the right side with the right sides facing one another. Repeat the process with patterned pieces.

* Attach the upper part of the handle with a 1/4 inch allowance, then sew toward the curves at the bottom of both pieces. Make

sure the handles are unlocked prior to securing both the sides of your neckline.

* Incorporate the solid pieces into the solid piece in the opposite direction by flipping it upside down. out. Then, insert them into the pattern piece. Cut the raw edges and align the seams and handles.

* Press all seams following making the bag right-side out to ensure that the side with the pattern is outside.

Fold the armholes, leaving an inch of space before pressing. Create baste stitches to hold them in place. Finish the handles by stitching one-quarter top stitch.

* Enjoy!

Superb Table Mats

What do you need:

* Fabric scissors

* 3x4 lightweight cotton canvas thread with contrasting shades

* Bone folder

* Leather adhesive

* Double-sided tape

* 12 square feet lambskin pieces

* Mat templates

Instructions:

* Make sure to increase the size of your templates by at minimum 300 percent prior to printing them out , and then cut out leather patterns. Cut 2 pieces to be the pattern's first symbol and then cut two pieces to have 4 pieces in your possession. Make use of 2 of the 4 pieces as templates for pattern 2.

* Take the canvas made of cotton then fold in half, then cut a section of the canvas towards the edges. Fold it in half and unfold it so that you have the reverse on the mat.

* Match two templates, then adhere them together using the double-adhesive tape.

* Sew the pieces by running stitches using a 1/8 inch seam allowance to create smoother flaps. Utilize a bone filer to open

the flaps , then make use of leather adhesive for glue.

* Allow 1/8 inch of headspace above the seam, and stitch top stitches over it.

Repeat the procedure with each of the other leather items, and be sure to attach similar pieces together applying double adhesive.

After that, lay the pattern of canvas you made earlier on the top of the lambskin leather mat and stitch them together with a an inch of allowance. You should leave an opening of about 10 inches on the opposite side of the design.

* Let the right side face upwards by turning the fabric upside down then , tuck in half an inch into the 10 inch gap you've made and then sew about 1/8 inch topstitches on the mat all the until the edge.

Washcloth Ducky

What do you need:

* Sponge

* Washcloth

* Thread

* Washcloth duck template

* Felt papers in orange and black

Instructions:

* Print template and expand it.

Cut out duck-shaped shapes of the template onto an old washcloth. Be sure you use solid lines so that you can make two ducks. One oval is the base. You will cut two similar shapes on the sponge to form the head, and two additional forms that will be used for tail. To make the body more robust, cut more sponge. You will then cut two additional shapes for the wings.

* Take two body pieces, then stitch them together, but make sure that you leave the bottoms open. fill it with sponges after flipping it right side out. Sew by hand after filling the hole with an oval piece and after that, sew the wings. Make sure to keep

the bottoms of the pieces open. Fill with sponges and sew the wings on by hand.

Make black knots of thread over the face to form eyes for the duck. Cut two oval-shaped pieces of felt paper to form the bill. Make use of the orange thread for stitching it onto.

The washcloth ducky is all set!

* Enjoy!

Gingham Coasters

What you require:

* Gingham scraps are divided into three 1/2-inch squares

* Vinyl with iron-on

Solid cotton scraps divided into three inch pieces

* Sewing equipment

* Sewing machine

Instructions:

* Pin gingham scraps to the scraps of cotton and leave the seam allowance of 1/2 inch.

* Apply vinyl to the gingham in accordance with the instructions on the packaging.

Trim edges, leaving 1/4 inch of space between seams.

* Enjoy!

iPod Case

What do you need:

* Needle and thread/sewing machines

* Fabric marker with erasable marking capabilities

* Mini scissors

* 9 3 to 5/8 inches fabric

* iPod cover design

Instructions:

* Download and print the iPod cover pattern , then cut the circular and rectangular holes.

* Pin the pattern onto the fabric. Use a pen to draw the openings and cut the openings out.

The fabric should be folded in two from one side to the other , then sew following pinning to keep it the fabric in the desired position. Make sure you leave 1/4 inch space.

* Enjoy!

Chapter 6: Easy Clothing Projects

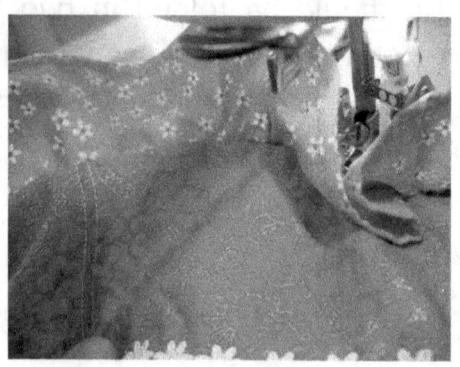

Then, of obviously, what better way to attempt making your own clothing? The projects for clothing in this section will amaze you and inspire you to give them a go for yourself.

Reusable Tunic for children

What you require:

* Fabric that has designs of your choice

* Thread

* Needles

* Scissors

* Tunic design

Double adhesive tape

Instructions:

First, ensure that you've washed and dried your fabric prior to making use of it.

* Download and print the pattern at 100%. Then use two adhesive tapes to adhere onto the cloth.

* You may also draw the pattern on the fabric with baking paper or the fabric chalk. This will mark the linings.

Cut the pieces in such a way that it is possible to have the top of the dress and the back the neck facing the sleeves, pockets and pocket lined pockets.

Make pleats on the neck by placing pleat lines onto the fabric, and then securing them to each other before sewing. Make use of slip stitches to stitch the pleats. Then, press them down.

* To create pockets, draw them using 5x1cm lines. Pin the lines that are marked to the center, and then press pleats along the sides from the folds at the top, all up to the folds at the bottom. Pin the linings on the center until you can see the rectangular portion inside the pocket. Sew around it leaving at least 3 cm of space prior to clipping and creating round edges. Make sure that the completed pocket will appear like the top edge was press-in, allowing you to quickly attach it to your dress. The dress should be pinched before sewing.

Then allow shoulder seams to come together by sewing the right and front seams together, then pressing them down.

Make the neckline by securing the neck overlock to the right and left sides of the neckline, then sewing around the neck's curve. Then, open one side up and leave 3cm of room before sewing the other pieces.

* To construct the sleeves, turn them and lock the sleeves over, then sew around the edge prior to pressing.

* Sew sleeves onto your dress using sewing them next to the curve. Bind the two rows.

* To sew the seam at the back put pins in the back, then stitch all the way to the button, pressing it down. After that, you can over-lock the button, leaving at least 2cm of room before using the iron to press.

* Sew everything up and then enjoy!

Ruffled Ombre Dress

What do you need:

Large piece cotton cloth

* Additional fabric for Ruffles

* Thread

* Needle

* Scissors

* Dress pattern

Instructions:

* Download and expand the pattern. About 100-300 percent will be sufficient.

* Trace the dress's design onto the fabric and cut the fabric.

Cut and fold however, make sure you're not overdoing it by cutting off the shoulders. Then create ruffles using lengths of cloth. It would be great to have different colors and stitch them onto the bodice's hem. Then, you can pin them to keep them in place. Make sure that you cut them at the back when needed. Make use of zigzag or running stitches for this task.

After that, put the back and front edges of your fabric together , and stitch the edges to create a single fabric.

Fold the edge in half and stitch a slip stitch to allow for an armhole.

* Next, you'll need additional material and make two pieces. Join them to make an extended strip.

* Sew the ends together . Make sure that you sew the bottom for the illusion that the piece is circular in its feel to it.

Make basting stitches for the strip of ruffles , then cover the strip by using an elastic strip, leaving the space of 1/4 inch. Make sure the elastic is sturdy enough to hold the dress.

* The opening will be the opening through which you can put the elastic. Expand it to the desired length prior to stitching the ends together, and then stitching through the opening in the casing.

Now you are wearing your ruffled ombre dress!

Loop T-Shirt Dress

What do you need:

* One shirt that perfectly fits you

* 1 larger t-shirt that can be cut

* Scissors

* Thread

* Needles

Instructions:

1. Put the smaller shirt over the larger shirt until you reach the neckline, then utilize the neckline as a indication of where to cut the fabric.

Cut the fabric until you have holes in the shoulders, sleeves and belled-out sides . Continue forward until you are able to have the shirt's hem visible.

* Using the pieces you cut off make two rectangle pieces which will later be used to create loops.

* Cut the rectangle pieces lengthwise in half and ensure that the opposite sides are close to each other. The edges should be sewn.

* Now, flip the fabric to the right.

Take the rectangular pieces of fabric and then loop them as you would tie a ribbon or knots. This gives the shirt some shape. Apply basting stitches to keep the loops together.

* Pin the front and back pieces together prior to sewing. Make sure you leave 1/4 inch of room. If you'd like to make it shorter, trim minimum 3 inches off the hem and you'll be good.

* Enjoy your new dress!

Halter Top Dress

What do you need:

* Halter top design

A large piece of fabric

* Scissors

* Thread

* Needle

* Iron

* Bias tape

Instructions:

* Increase the size of the pattern by 100%. Then download, print and trace it on the fabric. Make sure to add length, if necessary.

The shell is cut in half and then the liner from the fabric after you have pinned it down.

Cut some straps which are about 1.5 to 9 inches in dimension.

Cut a rectangle of fabric for the skirt. Then, add two inches of waist before cutting it and taking measurements to the desired length. Cut another shell for the underskirt , and increase the length by 2 inches in addition.

* Secure the straps to the shell, to the left and stitch the right sides together until the neck. This will strengthen the straps. Press then switch the fabric over right side up and press once more.

Make sure the sides are aligned with the back, then stitch with an elastic thread between lining as well as the edge in the shell.

* Sew a few baste stitches using a hand sewing needle or using a machine to secure the bottom.

* Secure the midpoint of straps to the neckline with bias tape. Fold bias tape to complete the strap.

Then, stitch parts of your skirt together with the shell, and the underskirt. Make sure you cover the lining with baste and ensure that both sides are facing upwards.

Sew any remaining edges and remove excess.

You now have a beautiful top-of-the-line dress!

Chapter 7: Where To Begin

Even though advanced technology has made it possible for quilts to be completed in the shortest amount of time, many of women remain loyal to the traditional method of quilting. Certain women are lucky enough to be able to start quilting with the guidance of a mentor who is more experienced like an elderly family member or a an individual in the community. However, for those who would like to learn how to quilt without guidance It can be difficult to determine a good starting point. For such people it is the best first step is to ensure that they have all the equipment necessary for quilting.

However, to have an accurate idea of what tools to pick up at the store, newbies need to first develop an understanding of the process of quilting works. The flow of quilting is simplified by the steps below:

1. Selection. This is the process of choosing the pattern and the design. Also,

it involves choosing the fabrics to choose and the batting to be used for part of the filling.

2. Measurement. The fabric will need to be measured to be matched with the pattern. This would also require breaking the fabric up into blocks which would be assembled to create an overall quilt pattern.

3. Layering. Sewing the blocks of fabric together is only the first step of quilting. Once the pieces are finished and are sewn in the backing needs to be sewn on. The batting will then be sandwiched between the two layers.

4. Sewing. Quilters can choose to stitch by hand or use a machine to stitch each layer of the quilt. Another layer that must be added to give the quilt a finishing finish is the binding that runs around each edge of the quilt. The binding is used to cover all edges to ensure that it doesn't look rough. It also holds the three layers together.

5. Trimming. This means trimming any excess thread, fabric, or any batting that is protruding from edge of quilt.

Understanding these steps helps anyone who is new to quilt understand that the equipment they will require to quilt include tools that allow for cutting, measuring and sewing.

Basic Terminology

If you're a person with some understanding of quilting, there's a good chance you've already figured out that the word "square" refers to the tiny block of fabric that's sewn to other blocks to make an overall quilt. The number of squares that are used is dependent on the quilt's size as well as the design. Other terms are important that could aid in understanding the method of quilting as well as find new patterns to apply.

In essence, quilting is the process of sewing by a series of layers of fabric to make a stunning piece like tablecloths as well as bed sheets or wall décor. The layers usually comprise a cloth top made of squares as well as a filling material that is placed at the center, as well as then a regular textile on the bottom. The layers are referred to as quilt sandwich.

The term"square"is commonly used to describe one block of fabric, the primary building block of a quilt."block." The term"block"is often used in order to mean an entire collection of nine squares sewn together to create an overall quilt. This can help simplify sewing the top piece made of a number of squares, which is called"the top of the quilt. If you've heard the term"piecing" is used, it refers to the procedure of sewn blocks, squares and other pieces to make a beautiful quilt top.

In the end, the most important terms you should be familiar with while you learn to quilt are:

Quilting is the method of stitching together multiple layers of fabric and other materials to create the quilt

Square is the building block of the quilt which is sewn with other squares in order to make an elongated block, and ultimately an end-to-end quilt top.

Block is a larger piece fabric that is made of nine smaller squares

The method of sewing squares or blocks together to form the top of a quilt.

The quilt top is the finished uppermost layer of the quilt made up of blocks and squares

Quilt sandwich refers to the three layers of the quilt including the top section and middle portion (composed from filling material) as well as the lower section (made from regular fabric or cloth)

The above terms are often employed in quilting discussion as well as guides and books. Therefore, it is important to learn about these terms so that it is easier for you to begin creating your first quilt in the near future.

What tools will you need to make the quilt?

Where can you get these equipment?

Chapter 8: Tools Required To Quilt

Before you begin quilting You must ensure that you've got everything necessary to complete the job correctly. You can purchase several of the tools required for a successful quilt at a local retailer, but you could look into specialty shops and ask the salesperson to ensure that you have the correct equipment or tools for your quilting endeavor.

Every artist requires tools for creating amazing works. Quilting is no exception. Anyone who wants to make stunning quilts that can be handed down through generations should be equipped with the following tools in their arsenal:

Sewing Machine

The first thing a quilter will require is a sewing device, however, this would not be required when she's already proficient at sewing by hand. But those who aren't enough confident in their hand-sewing skills will need to purchase an equipment for sewing. The sewing machine you purchase doesn't need to be costly as it's excellent and it is able to do the job properly.

Furthermore, some of the more expensive sewing machines are fitted with unique stitch designs. This isn't necessary because quilting usually requires the simple straight stitch. The top-end machines may be quite complex for those who are just beginning. Based on reviews from users and suggestions from other professional seamstresses, novices should consider the following features when choosing the sewing machine they are planning to purchase:

The price is affordable – as stated, the price of sewing machines depends on the features offered by it. When choosing between various models of sewing machines for basic use, it's usually best to choose ones that are a bit more expensive than the others. Because these machines tend to be more durable than their competitors and offer better warranties on service.

* Simple to use. The most important factor for beginners is the ease at the sewing machine could be threaded. The reason is that incorrect threading can cause problems with the thread when the machine is operating. This can result in breaking, bunching, or looping. The majority of machines have step-by-step instructions on how to spin the bobbin before running it through the needle. Be sure to follow these steps precisely to avoid having to have any problems at any time.

* Reliable simply means that the sewing machine must be able to perform as it has been promised. The machine you choose for quilting must be able to create the same quality stitches across multiple fabrics.

Scissors

They are essential for any kind of sewing job. One thing you should keep in mind about cutting scissors for sewing is that they that are used to cut fabric should not be used to cut other non-fabric materials.

This could cause the edges to become dull on the scissors, rendering them ineffective to cut fabric. This is particularly true if the scissors used for cutting fabric are to cut paper. Because quilting involves cutting fabric as well as paper designs and patterns, it's best having two pair of scissors to serve every purpose.

Another option is to mark each set of scissors according to the purpose for which it was intended or simply buy scissors that have different colors of handles.

Ironing Board

Similar to the sewing machine an ironing board doesn't have to be an expensive item. In fact, novices could use the ironing board they already have in their home. However, experts quilters often complain that the shapes of the ironing boards they have at home do not meet their requirements with regard to how they iron quilt materials. This is why the majority of quilters choose to purchase a larger boards or get their current boards customized to suit their needs.

The ironing boards which best fit the quilting process are usually bigger than normal boards. The width will be constant from one end to the next this gives the board an overall shape that is more rectangular when compared with regular boards. This board can be paired with a heavy iron that can produce steam.

Other essential items you'll require for quilting include several spools of thread an edge ripper, as along with needles and pins.

Rotary Cutters

For some, it may be difficult to understand why a cutter is needed even if they already have scissors for fabric in their possession. It is important to remember that rotary cutters have differently than scissors. Scissors can be used to cut curved patterns onto any kind of fabric and also for cutting and trimming. But, it's faster to utilize a rotary cutter in cutting straight lines on rectangular pieces of material to be used for quilting. This is particularly useful to cut a whole distance of material in a straight line.

Selecting the best type of rotary cutter could be difficult for many beginners. That's why the majority of beginners are forced to buy Rotary cutters that come in a range of sizes. For those in a budget purchasing multiple cutters won't be a good idea. In this instance it is possible to settle for an rotary cutter that comes with 45 millimeter blade. The majority of quilters believe this to be the right size to cut quilt fabrics. Beginners need not be concerned about cutting the quilt layers apart even if they finish up with the same dimensions with the stitches on both sides.

The 45mm blade rotary cutter is designed to slice through two to three layers of fabric, including the batting. Of of course, using the rotary cutter is also using the cutting mat. This will ensure that the surfaces of tables and floors aren't damaged. A ruler is necessary to have with the rotary cutter, to ensure your cut stays smooth and precise. When cutting quilts, it is best to select the rulers designed specifically to be used for quilting. These rulers are available in various sizes and are made to assist in cutting different lengths of quilting fabric. The purchase of rulers in all sizes is considered to be a worthwhile investment by quilters who are skilled.

Cutting Mat

The mat for cutting is typically 18 inches wide by 24 inches long, and should be marked prior to use to make it more straightforward cutting squares. Some quilters like to use eyeballs for the process, however for those who are new to quilt, I strongly suggest purchasing mats. It can be used as a cutting board for your cloth that can be a wonderful tool to use when you're using a Rotary cutter. There are larger boards, and based on your requirements you might want to think about buying an extra-large table.

However, for the beginning the size listed above will suffice.

Bias Tape Marker

An excellent tool is a 2-inch bias tape marker, which will assist you mark the fabric to cut. Make sure you don't use a marker while cutting the fabric prior to cutting it, because the ink might be absorbed and cause damage to the fabric. Instead, use bias tape to mark your requirements.

Thread

There are two kinds of threads that are suitable for quilting two types of threads: clear and white nylon. These threads are utilized to seal seams or to attach various fabrics to quilts or work on corners. Always ensure you be using thread when quilting. These threads are great when you're making a quilt using bright colors and you want something that is durable but not too evident.

Fabric

Although the fabric you select entirely dependent on your preferences I strongly suggest you purchase some cotton fabrics. It is a breeze that is easy to use, it's soft and extremely durable. It also becomes soft when you wash it. This is something you won't get with other kinds of fabrics. Additionally, many fabrics tend to tear when cut, however it is cotton that's the best choice for delicate designs and patterns.

Seam Ripper

Although sharp scissors are able to accomplish the task however, it's also a good idea to purchase an seam ripper. It is a tool employed to remove stitches. It has a curved blade that has a sharp point end. The opposite edge has a ball to protect the surrounding fabric from damage. Seam rippers come in various sizes, ranging between 1.75 inch to six inches. They are also available with different styles of handles and colors.

After you have all the tools in place It's time to begin the quilt's layout.

Chapter 9: Everything About Quilt Blocks

The quilt block can be described as the fundamental element that makes up the upper layer. Every quilt block gets sewn into and joined to another block. The process continues until the top layer is finished. Before the blocks are created there are a number of elements that must be taken into consideration first. This includes:

1. The pattern. Many expert quilters suggest geometric patterns for novices. This is because creating geometric shapes such as squares and triangles from cloth is a lot simpler. It's also simple to stitch these shapes together to create an appealing pattern.

Another quilting design that can be simple for novices to create is by sewing strips of fabric together. The strips can be sourced from various clothing items that are otherwise discarded.

2. The dimensions of the piece. A quilt's size generally depends on the purpose it is going to be employed for. If it's going to be used for bedding material, then you'll be required to know the size of the bed. Bed sizes usually include twin, king, queen or double beds. This means that the bedding material must be large enough to completely cover the bed and leave a bit additional on the sides that can be put into the frame in the event of need.

Also, the dimensions of a table topper will also depend on how big the table is. Quilts to be used as table runners typically must be 11-12 inches in width as well as 15-18 inches in length. Quilts to be used as wall decors should be at minimum 9 inches square, or more than the size. It is possible to apply the same method when determining the dimensions of a quilt that will be suitable for the crib, baby's bed, pillows and pillowcases and so on.

Building the Blocks

After having all the equipment and understanding about the various aspects to be considered first, the next step to be done is to figure out how to make a queen-sized quilt.

Be aware that when creating the quilt, you can't simply pedal to your sewing machine in hopes to complete the quilt in one go. Instead, you must build it in sections. For those who are new to the craft, I suggest using a nine-square pattern that is comprised consisting of three rows of squares stacked on top of each other. So, you'll have three squares in the lower row and three at the center and finally three on top. It is recommended to trace this pattern prior to sewing together to ensure that you be able to see the work you've done.

Once these squares are assembled, you are able to effortlessly join them to make a quilt. If you use a standard size that is 3.5 inches by 3.5 inches for each piece each square will measure 10.5 inches. A queen-sized quilt of basic size is around eight squares x six squares.

You are free to pick the material you wish to utilize. You can choose to use the traditional buck, or an applique, or go imaginative. Keep in mind that you are making your quilt So, you're free to choose whatever you feel is right. Beginners can make it easier by using a simple double-color design. But , ultimately, this depends on the style you prefer.

The most inexpensive and easy fabric for the quilting process is cotton. Most fabric stores have enough cotton fabrics that are ready to go, which you can purchase for lower prices or offer it for the fabric for free.

If you're still learning about quilting it's recommended to get some of these before you invest in a high-quality piece of material. Sometimes, you'll discover a huge amount of fabric that is perfect to learn. There is even an pattern that you've never attempted working with before.

For a perfect quilt it is necessary to make 48 blocks in nine pieces which means you must make the fabric in 432 squares. It may be overwhelming however, when you arrange the blocks into different shades, it's easier to use. For instance, it's simple to make up to 70 squares out of one yards of material. Therefore, approximately 5 yards is enough for a queen-sized quilt. There's plenty of squares left for the event that you make mistakes.

After you've made your squares The following step will be to select the stuffing material. There are many options to choose from and in the end there's no ideal material. Different materials can provide your quilt with different styles, so you might be able to spend some time to experiment with the materials you would like to have the best.

The most commonly used material for stuffing is cotton due to its texture, and because it is very easy for you to manipulate. It is more breathable when in comparison to other fabrics and it is easy to lay it flat. It's also extremely comfortable and lasts a long time.

Another fabric you can utilize is polyester. While it's more affordable in comparison to cotton, you will encounter a few negatives with this material. It can get tangled in the quilt, especially after repeated washing and may even show through the fabric. This isn't ideal for an edgy or dark quilt as it's appearance may be worn. However, when you want to provide warmth it is a suitable material to use over cotton in the middle part of your quilt.

Wool is also used to stuff. This is the largest and warmest fabric and is therefore ideal when you're making a queen-sized quilt to be used in winter. But, it can be a major problem in terms of cleaning because it is heavier when wet, and can also shrink. Therefore, dry cleaning is the best. In addition, wool is more difficult to work with since it is difficult to bend and flatten.

You will also have to locate the fabric for the bottom portion and the sheet that is behind it. It is possible to choose a huge sheet of fabric, but you can purchase an already-sewn piece from the local store selling textiles. The color will depend on what you prefer, while white is the best option for quilts.

Chapter 10: Making Your First Quilt:

Step By Step Guide

Are you ready to start the first piece of quilting? This chapter will provide you with a the steps to follow.

Step 1: Begin with the Squares

The first step in making an ideal quilt would be to start using the squares. It is essential to have a straight ruler to guide your cutting. This will help you avoid making a lot of errors. If your cutter is brand new it could cut four pieces using just one fold of fabric. Be assured that you won't be worried if you've damaged an edge or the cuts you cut are uneven. In some cases, this happens with the roller which is a little dull. It's easy to repair those edges during your sewing procedure.

It is possible to use fabric scissors alternatively, if you do not prefer the Rotary cutter. It could be a little more difficult to cut with scissors if also have to work on flat boards. Be extra cautious and make certain to make use of a bias tape draw lines.

No matter what cutting tool you are using, ensure to keep the squares close to take them out when you need they. Additionally, it can be very easy to forget the quantity of fabric you've already cut so having them by your disposal is extremely helpful.

Step 2 Lay out the squares

The process of laying out the squares is vital before making the squares. This allows you to observe the pattern and identify any obvious mistakes on your squares.

When piecing the squares together make sure you provide an allowance for seams of 1/4 inch. This is essential and failing to provide this space could result in an unfinished quilt. If you prefer using pins to secure the pieces in to the front, you may do this, but when you've practiced quilting you'll see that you have to spend a lot of time pins, time that you could use to do actual quilting.

The best method to avoid making mistakes when piecing the squares is to work on only a single row of pieces at one time. This will give you pieces that are simple to join, and also allows you to view for each line where the quilt is moving. It is important to make sure that seams are stitched in a flat fashion. This will result in the amazing quilt you've got in your head.

The most common concern is ironing out every square. Do not stress about it now, because you can iron these blocks out later. The process of pre-washing is also unproductive since you will be able to clean the quilt after you're done. Pre-washing may also make the fabric more difficult to work with as well, which is not something you would want to do to do for your first quilt.

If you'd like to keep your seams flat and even, the best option is to flip the pieces over and flatten them with your fingers. This is a quick and quick way to smooth the seam. The seam will allow you to put your quilt stays in place perfectly. Be aware that there's no need to spend your time by individually pressing the squares at this moment.

Step 3- Work on the 1/4-inch seam allowance

It is the next thing to do: focus on the nagging but crucial seam allowance. The majority of sewing machines have a the 1/4 inch foot is available, but in the event that your machine doesn't include this feature, this is an affordable item to purchase at your local craft shop.

If you aren't able to search for the item an ordinary masking tape is an option as long as you are patient. Another factor to think about is the 1/4 inch seams is to rely on the sewing equipment. It is recommended to measure your needle, not from the grid. It may be beautiful and attractive, but it may be wrong. Quilters rely on their own measurements.

Step 4: Iron the Blocks

After you have sewn every block of nine then you must lay them out so that you can see the final appearance of the quilt. This will be your best opportunity to press your blocks so that you can complete the entire process in one go.

Step 5-Finish the Step 5-Finish the

It is essential to lay the blocks at least once before you are able to finalize your pattern. This will help you determine the areas where you're not getting something in your design or if you have incorrect sizes of your blocks. Additionally, it can help you put the blocks together a little easier if you are aware of where each piece is supposed to go.

Additionally, you could employ a masking tape label the blocks you're working on. This can be helpful if you are working with blocks and put them in an orderly pile. By marking the row and column they is to be placed in can be extremely helpful to making sure that they stay in their appropriate locations.

Step 6: Join the Blocks

When you are piecing the blocks together it is best to work on a single column at one time. Note that the issue comes when you be working with a lot of fabric. This is why you must make sure to roll the seams to help you. Once you're done it is possible to press the blocks to smooth the seams and fabric. The blocks must appear as seamless as you can to make the fabric ready to proceed with the subsequent step. This can be very difficult.

Step 7: Sew the top Quilt

In piecing the top of the quilt it is recommended to utilize pins. It is best to give enough space between 2 and three squares. However, this is contingent on your preferences. If you don't pin the fabric the blocks could move and may be difficult to stitch. After you've put in lots of effort to this point, this might not be the final thing you'd like to happen to your quilt.

You may need to set the fabric on your lap while working on it, but it's vital to finish the edges of your quilt also. It will look beautiful and also extend the longevity of your quilt when you trim the areas that could become worn out. Keep your 1/4-inch seam and make sure to keep the edge while you work. Trim the edges, if necessary. After you've finished then you can iron the edges. The top quilt is finished!

Chapter 11: Connecting The Back Of The Quilt

You are now ready to put the quilt on your back. This is the most difficult part and you should take your time on this one. The first step is to make sure you have a level, clean surface on which to be productive. Also, ensure that your feet and hands are clean. It is important to walk on your quilt, and you shouldn't make the quilt filthy. Lay the top quilt out and put in the stuffing material. Then, finish it off with your back quilt, and begin sewing.

There aren't enough pins to complete this task. It is necessary to make three layers. These layers will eat up quite a bit once you begin sewing. Three layers is the ideal amount to begin with, but you are always able to add more layers. Make sure you smooth the stuffing material in the process and keep an eye on wrinkles or tears while you work. Keep in mind that it's much simpler to re-pin a seam than re-sew.

Most of the time there will be a time when a piece of the quilt may get tangled, which can happen while you are moving around the. Therefore, you must be more inventive when the quilt you are making. You will need an object of weight to bring down the sheets before flaying the sheets. Make sure you make use of a large number of pins.

When you're done with the pinning, you will need to examine the needles and the thread. It is possible to choose a thread of cotton that matches the color of the sheet on the bottom to make the under stitch and clear nylon thread for the top stitch.

I highly suggest that you test a number of stitches on a spare fabric prior to beginning to make sure that your machine is properly calibrated as well as that your stitch pattern is aligned. Be aware that it's more beneficial to discover that you're using a defective needle on a test piece rather than on your quilt.

Since you're working on three different layers of fabric and three layers of fabric, it is best to use the use of a walking foot. This will make the job easier and help in reducing the tendency to bunch. Start with the outer long edge and begin working on the long edges by rolling the quilt while doing so.

Once you've reached the halfway point take the quilt off and then turn it over to begin on the opposite side. Make sure you keep moving throughout your work and don't hurry. Be patient and remember that there is no need to move straight from one side to the next while you select your rows.

If you're done with length, you can now begin to tackle the width. This is slightly simpler, as you will have a smaller space to work with. When done correctly the final seam will be a straight thin line between the quilt blocks. After a quick ironing, your quilt is finished.

Chapter 12: Proper Edging

You'll notice that the edges of the quilt might appear worn. It is possible to improve this with a proper edge, this will help not just make your quilt attractive but also help to make it stronger.

Begin the edging by binding the corners. By using tape, make a mark approximately 2 inches in width and cut strips approximately 3.75 inches (length). Cut about 8 pieces from these. The corners should be folded at 45 degrees. Secure with pins, and then begin sewing.

Now, you'll need a bias tape marker as well as longer strips. Start working on the reverse part of the strip so that you see the stitching and to keep it level. After that, begin flattening the seams with your fingers. Make sure to flip it over before working on the opposite side.

Always use bias tape and make sure that you've got everything perfectly in accordance with your preferences.

Rework the quilt's main piece to make sure that edges are cut and even. Make use of the fabric scissors to align the quilt and ensure that edges are straight.

Unfasten the side of the bias tape, then place the edge along the edges of your quilt. Include a pin 6 inches to secure the pieces to each other. Then fold over and then pin the remainder. The corners may require an extra effort, and there are a variety of ways to enhance their appearance. Use the triangle fold to aid in helping the sewing machines to make it easier to match how you sew. However, keep in mind the fact that it's a fashion preference, and it is entirely your choice.

When you're ready to sew, change to the normal foot and make a note of removing the pins as well as the tape while you sew. If you prefer to do a double stitch, feel free to do so. Be aware that this is your edge. A large part of the job is to sew the pieces while ensuring that the quilt looks attractive.

Once you've put the edges in place and then return to your running foot and fold in the corners and get ready to continue running in a single line. It's fine to stop after a while However, be sure to be aware of what this might look like in different angles.

Chapter 13: Why You Should Learn Sewing

Sewing was a skill was traditionally reserved for women and homemakers who were taught. In the present, much has changed, and everyone is eager to master as many important techniques as they can, especially when it means they can make their lives better. Sewing is a wonderful technique to learn for many reasons not only to ensure that you can quickly repair your clothes, but additionally to take pleasure in the joy of developing your creativity and creating new clothing.

Sewing is also a technique which can assist you in saving moneysince buying clothing can be expensive. Also, you can count on the therapeutic aspect of sewing. You start a project with a mess of loose ends that don't work together and finish the job with a piece which looks stunning. There are other reasons you might like to try sewing.

1. To discover your own independence: If you're in a position to design your own clothes, you can enjoy some degree of independence. If you are required to go to a party or require a particular outfit at short notice it is not a problem in trying to locate an open shop or a place to make an purchase. It is easy to design the outfit you'd like to wear, making sure you have an individual look in a flash.

2. Sewing is a great way to conserve the environment. Sewing provides you with an chance to reuse materials and make unique products to serve a variety of needs. This means you don't have to buy new materials or to throw away any you already have that could be suitable for a different item. Curtains can easily be transformed into cushions, or an worn-out pair of jeans can make a fantastic shirt that comes and a bag to match. This is all possible in the event that you are able to sew.

3. Sewing is economical Sewing can not only help you save money, but also time

and effort when making clothes. There are many other things you can sew. You can make unique objects to be used in the decoration of your house, like tablescloths and curtains, and you can also make a variety of craft projects. You can make a great sewing. You don't have to think about buying gifts for your loved ones and you can design customized gifts in a matter of minutes.

4. Sewing allows you to develop your own unique style: A lot of people prefer to have an individual look that is distinctive and allows them to stand out as distinct. Being able to sew lets you define your ideal way to appear to ensure that you don't have to worry about whether you look like someone else when you leave your house. If you have clothing that you bought previously and you are able to see that it is easy to alter your clothes to make them more suitable for you with the right knowledge of sewing.

5. Sewing lets you replicate the look of an amazing design for a dress on a runway ,

but you realize that you can't afford to buy it? If you're able to sew, you are able to examine it and get inspiration to make your own clothing that is identical. In addition, most clothes are designed in sizes which are typical for models, however they may not be appropriate for the person who will wear it. If you are able to sew, you'll be able to ensure that you make clothes that flatter you across your body, so you can get you look the best of your body.

6. Be a rebel against stereotypes: The times have changed, and more men are getting into sewing, as evident by the countless clothes makers who share their collections. Today, sewing means to explore your creative side, and gender discrimination is rapidly fading away.

7. Sewing abilities will remain useful: Regardless of the location you are anywhere in the world and no matter what your status in society is, being able to sew is always an advantageous. It is because all people require clothing to

cover their bodies and also utilize this skill to earn income.

8. Sewing is a great feeling: Once you've finished the sewing project you had been working on, you'll feel an immense sense of satisfaction and will feel proud having accomplished your task. The best part is to wear your creation when you go out and get applause for it. Since it is a skill is a process that will improve with practice and time. Before you are sure of you're capable of creating anything you need in the event that the materials are available, including a thread and needle.

If you decide to learn how to sew and you discover that there are plenty of benefits you will get from it. Sewing is an art that is useful in its nature which means that you'll discover that you can use it in many scenarios, no matter if you're trying to create something completely fresh, or to fix an item which has sustained damage.

Chapter 14: Equipment And Devices Needed For Sewing

It is true that tools can make art more evident. This means that no matter what the art or task you're performing, you have to have access to the necessary devices and tools. There are times when a person is competent and has all the skills, but there are some limitations because of non-functional devices and equipment, making it difficult for someone to display his talents.

Sewing is an entirely machine-driven process. It requires from the person sewing that the equipment is examined for the correct operation to ensure that all sewing tasks are performed seamlessly and without any errors. Here are a few of the items you'll require in case you are keen to master about the craft of sew.

Sewing machine: It is a machine that is used for sewing fabrics and other materials by using thread. The majority of people prefer using machines rather than sewing by hand since it is significantly faster and more neat. Sewing machines are highly favored by those who want to sew commercially since it is simpler to make a standard product.

Sewing Shears: They are available in various types. The shears with a bent handle are about 7 inches long and can be used to cut fabrics. Because the blades are perfectly on their cutting surfaces. The pinking shears , on the other hand, cut with a zigzag line. They are thus suitable to finish hem edges and seams. They should not be used to cut the fabric as they do not provide a precise cut line for the fabric. All shears must be exceptionally sharp or else they could create irreparable injury to your fabric which will be cut.

Measurement mats made of cardboard This tool allows you to cut patterns or pieces of material when you're preparing the pieces to stitch. Additionally, it can be used to provide protection to the surface you're cutting on to ensure that there isn't any injury caused by sharp edges of cutting tools.

Trimming Scissors These are 6-inch long scissors used to trim seams and clip them. They're lighter than sheers and are designed to cut through materials that are a significant amount smaller. Similar to the shears, they must be razor-sharp. They're multi-purpose and are also able to cut other items that have to do with the sewing process.

Tailor's Chalk Tailor's Chalk thin piece of chalk used in tailoring to make permanent alteration marks on clothes. It is able to help the tailor determine the spot where he should stitch a cut piece of fabric. It can easily be wiped off, meaning that you don't have to worry about whether there will be marks left behind that could impact the end result.

Needles - These are available in a variety of sizes, including various widths, lengths and sizes. They can also be classified into three primary kinds: the medium, small, or large size needles. Small needles are commonly used on lightweight and soft fabrics like silk, which is delicate and big needles are designed for dense, rough and heavy fabrics like tweed or wool. Needles are used to bast, sew buttons and for repairing tears in clothing. They are generally used in handwork. Sewing machines also include needles since they are needed to ensure that the thread stays in place and holds the cloth in place. There are needles employed for decorative tasks like embroidery.

A tracing wheel is a tool with two teeth on a wheel , as well as the handle. The teeth may be either smooth or serrated. A tracing wheel is used for various purposes during sewing. These include:

It's employed to transfer patterns onto fabrics. It can be utilized with the tracing tapper, or even without. The marks you can transfer from patterns include pleats and darts buttonholes, pocket placement lines and appliques.

It also creates slotted perforations. This allows you to sew along a line in order to ensure that sewing is not uneven.

Dressmaker's carbon papers - This is used in conjunction with the tracing wheels and it works in like normal carbon paper. It comes in a variety of shades. If you're looking at creating marks that are subtle, it is recommended to use this over the chalk for tracing.

Tape measure or measuring tape It is typically measured in a 60 inch length device utilized to record measurements of your body, to draw patterns, as well as for measuring fabrics. The flexible and soft tape measure works best. If you come across someone who is proficient at sewing, they'll usually have their tape measure right to them, hung loosely around their neck. This is because they utilize the tape measure often.

Iron box and smaller ironing boards for all flat surfaces. You'll need an iron box in order to eliminate wrinkles from fabric or completed project in order to make it appear tidy. The ironing board must be lightweight, compact in size, and resistant to heat. To iron during the sewing process the process, it's best to utilize a dry iron box rather than steam iron boxes.

Sturdy thread - Thread which is extremely light may result in a jam on the machine because it's more prone to becoming knotted. Furthermore, it is prone to be easily broken, resulting in repetition of threading.

The seam ripper (an absolute necessity to remove the stray stitches and unsightly seams). Always handle it carefully as it could endanger the fabric.

Straight pins that are small to medium size. They can be very helpful when cutting and sewing materials. They can help keep things in place, preventing the possibility of making mistakes when cutting. Beware of pins that are dull and pointed and which are rusty, they can end up ruining your fabric.

A Pin Cushion - This is a cushion made of cotton that is cut and sewn into many different designs. It can be useful in keeping the pins in their place. It can help you work more efficiently when it is placed on your waist , especially when you're doing a job which requires many pins.

Yardstick, also known as a Meter stick- It is employed to measure fabric length and to verify the grain lines. It is also employed to mark a straight line, and for measuring lengths of hems. It will be required once you have begun to develop your sewing abilities.

Cutting table- Also known as"the cutting bar. It is necessary to put an unflat board on a table to serve as a cutting table. This is where you'll lay your fabric to cut. You can then pin your fabric to the board for ease of cutting. This will allow you to precisely cut it into the desired shape.

L-square It will be handy when you're constructing perpendicular lines by using divisional components that are situated in shorter and longer arms.

Ruler: This can help you connect the smaller lines you've drawn in centimeters or inches.

Sewing Gauge: It measures from 6 to 8 inches. It comes with a movable indicator, which helps to measure shorter lengths.

Hem Gauge Hem Gauge of measurement device identified with various thicknesses and folds in the hem. It is helpful when you need to hem edges of grain straight.

Hip CurveIt is utilized to create a shape and connect points that have a slight curvature. Similar to measuring tape, this one has inches measurement on the front, and centimeter measurements on the reverse.

Beeswax or Candle is a great way to strengthen your thread. It is also utilized as a lubricant to make the thread more comfortable to use when you're working with hand-sewing tasks, like sewing with buttons.

Sewing Box- This can serve as a toolbox for tailors of all kinds. Sewing equipment like pins threads, thimbles, and many more are kept in this container so you will always have the items you require. Sewing boxes are different and they vary in style, such as the compartmentalized and non-compartmentalized box. A sewing box that is compartmentalized is useful because all your sewing equipment can be well-organized. You require one to ensure that you do not get rid of anything you need for the new sewing venture.

Thimble is a crucial instrument in sewing. It could be made of metallic or plastic. It is used for hand sewing to ensure that your finger is safe from needles poking. It is necessary to have a thimble that fits to ensure that you can sew comfortably. It can also increase your confidence as you're confident that the needle won't cause harm to you.

Emery Bag- You will utilize this bag to thrust your pins and needles. It will sharpen your needles and pins as well as remove corrosion, if it exists. So you won't need to be concerned about causing damage to your sewing materials sewing.

A tailor's Ham - This is also known as "a dressmaker's" Ham. It resembles an oversized pillow that is the shape of a ham and is stuffed tightly. It's utilized to create a mold for to press on curves such as collars and sleeves.

Chapter 15: Sewing Machine And Its Basics

The sewing machine is at the core of sewing. As a beginner, you should know everything about this tool, which will assist you in making your sewing more efficient and precise.

The essential components of a machine to sew include the following:

1. Power Switch

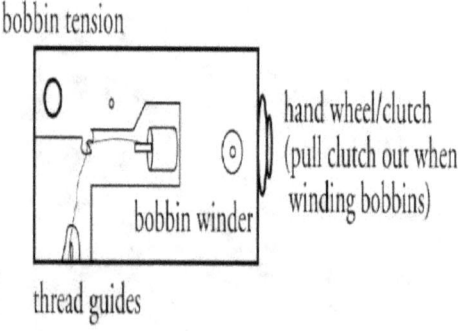

The power switch could be in different alignments, based on the model of machine. The power switch is the point of connection of the power source to machine that can turn the machine either on or out. The power and light switches are distinct. If children are present in the area in which the machine is located in, it's a sensible alternative to keep the switch shut for greater safety. If the machine does not have a power supply, the security procedures can be improved by using the safety strip that connects to the power source.

2. Light

Access to a good light is vital to ensure a successful sewing. The position of the light is dependent on the type of machine. Certain machines include multiple light locations. However, the light in the needle's area and the pressure foot are extremely important. The light could connect to the supply of power, or occasionally it is not and operated by battery power.

3.

Stitches

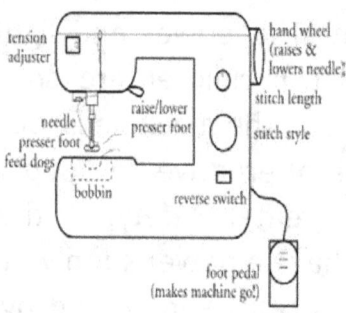

Each sewing machine comes with a variable amount of stitches to be selected depending on the time of need. Thus, selecting the right stitch is important. There are a variety of stitches available that are straight for sewing traditional fashion while decorative stitches are used for different kinds of pattern making. Making the best choice of stitch for the correct style of dress can make your stitching exceptional. The main elements include straight, blind hem,

Zigzag, buttonhole, and Mending stitches are the main varieties. The reverse stitching technique can be used to fix the seams. As a starting point, is required, you must know the the stitch length and width capacities.

To create unique decorative possibilities There are many machines that offer an array of decorative stitches. Although they have a variety of stitches, they cannot ensure the performance of the machine. If you're just beginning to learn, it is possible to start with the basic stitches, even if they are fewer.

4. Display Screen

Modern digital sewing machines come with an LCD display screen or LED that allows users to select the tension adjustment as well as the choices for stitching. The secret to the perfect stitch is maintaining the tension of the lower and upper threads. Certain digital machines provide the option of having numbers on the dials that are external to allow for alteration of the tension of the upper. For manual machines, it has to be manually adjusted. For the bobbin thread, tension can be adjusted by screws on the casing of the bobbin.

5. Presser Feet

In the beginning, you have to be aware of how many presser feet are included with the model of your machine. The fundamental kinds of presser feet are:

Multi-purpose feet are designed to stitch straight stitches and stitch in zigzag patterns for sewing basics.

Zipper foot

Buttonhole foot

Blind Hem Foot

Teflon shoe for fabric that is sticky

The decorative stitch feet

Hemming feet that are narrow

and hundreds more based on the model of the machine

There are several kinds for presser foot. There are brand-specific Feet that are only available through a dealer, and the generic ones, which you can purchase from idea companies or from the fabric stores. It is easy to handle both of these feet using your machine, as long as you are aware of what the reason for the feet.

Many machines offer the ability to change the pressure of foot presser, which means that any type of fabric thin or thick, is easily adjustable for both thin and thick fabric. Certain machines also have extra lifting space, so you can effortlessly put in thicker fabric.

6. Thread Delivery

One of the most important instruments of sewing machines are the spool pins that serve to secure thread. Sewing machines are equipped with multiple numbers of horizontal and vertical spools. Metallic and novelty threads typically require rotating positioning to feed the thread without binding or sliding. If your sewing machine has several spools pin It will allow you to utilize more than one needle in order that various designs can be created. This information is typically found in the user manuals of sewing machines.

7. Bobbins

The sewing machine is equipped with an bobbin, which is the primary source of the stitches. Certain machines have the ability to take the bobbin home, however, others might not have this feature. The amount of thread inside the bobbin could be detected through the sensors built into the machine. The sensors will let you detect when the bobbin's thread is empty of thread. Also, if the bobbin is full, the sensor will notify you. The sensors enable seamless stitching, ensuring that stitching does not get cut off due to a lack of thread.

8. Needle Position

Digital and computerized sewing machines come with the option of adjustment of several needle positions. This is crucial for those who want to change your stitching line in different directions while keeping your fabric at the same width. It is important to know how to adjust the needle's position depending on the width of fabric.

Selecting the right sewing machine

There are a myriad of sewing machines you can pick from. There are the expensive ones and the more expensive models, basic sewing machines that include reverse and forward options, computers which can be used to embroider large patterns and many more designs. This is why it can be difficult for a novice who would like to begin sewing but is on a tight budget to buy a high-quality sewing machine without having to go through some confusion. But, there are a few things to consider that can assist you in getting started:

1. Think about the reason you've got to use the sewing machine. What kind of projects do you wish to tackle? If you are looking to perform repairs and modifications then you must select an

alternative sewing machine to the tailor who wants to work on quilting or embroidery.

2. Take note of the amount of time you'll spend on the sewing machines. Are you going to be using it for something you'll use more frequently or just occasionally during the week?

3. Do you need a simple machine or a top-of-the-line machine? For beginners sewing machine, a basic one is ideal, but when you intend to work on a larger scale after you have mastered the basics, you'll need to purchase the right machine to accomplish a bit more.

4. First, shop as many that you are able to. It is important to be aware of the products available and what it is. Online shopping is the most convenient way to purchase today because you will be able to easily check out what's readily available, and where it's accessible and all the details about each available sewing machine. In addition, it can save you lots of time shopping on the internet.

5. If you're shopping within a tight budget then you must write the kinds of equipment are affordable. It is best to choose the best of all.

Chapter 16: The Fundamental Sewing Techniques

Once we've taken our journey a little simple by examining the main ideas of sewing and tools and equipment that go with it We can now focus our attention on the main sewing techniques. The methods discussed here are typically the most commonly used sewing techniques.

Sewing fundamentals: the essentials of sewing

The basic principle for sewing is that you join the opposite side to each other. The right side is that which is the final side of your dress, or accessory. It is a good rule of thumb that the right side will usually be more attractive and shiny. If you follow these rules, then the messy appearance of your stitches won't be visible and the dress, or any other piece you are stitching will have a neat appearance.

The seam allowance refers to the distance between stitch and edge of fabric. The standard length is usually 1/4 inches. However, it's not a standard and the key thing to remember is that whichever seam allowance you decide to use for your stitching should be calculated well prior to the time you can cut that estimated length for your fabric. This means that seam allowances let you cut your fabric to the appropriate length.

Begin stitching

The first step is to look at diagrams of straight seams

1.

Begin with straight seams and to do this, you'll will require your cloth or fabric and fold it on the right sides.

2. Put the item on the machine in such an arrangement so to ensure that both the pressing foot and folded edges are aligned with one another. This will allow you to create a precise seam allowance.

3. Then turn around the wheels of the device so that it faces the needle on the bottom and then towards the scrap.

4.

The next step is the presser foot. Place it in place using the lever located at the back. Be sure that when you begin sewing, the presser foot is in the down position. This will let you get a steady and smooth sewing and the fabric will automatically go to the machine. It is all you need is a little assistance in changing the fabric.

5. Following that, you need pressing the pedal on your foot so that the stitch can move forward.

6. The reverse button on your machine will allow you to stitch some stitches in reverse. In this situation, you do not

require a knot at the top of your stitch. Your stitch will stay secured and secure.

7.

Continue stitching forward until you get to the outside that the material. Repeat the process of stitching backwards before stitching forward. During this procedure you must keep the needle in its most elevated level so that it will not be able to unthread.

8. When you're done with the forward and backward stitching of the fabric take it off the machine and take it untidy of the sewing machine. To do this, you'll need elevate the presses feet. When you are removing the fabric, ensure that you have cut off all the waste thread from the edge of the fabric this way.

These extra threads won't interfere with the next sewing.

Turn your cloth over to the right and admire the beautiful seam. If you ever find that you are unable to finish your seam exactly as you would like make sure you have your seam ripper close by, so you can achieve what you desire.

Swirling up and down the Corners

If you're sewing any type of dress or stitch a different accessory, you might not always be able to get the exact straight seam. If that were the case, sewing would have become extremely laborious and time demanding. We'll now proceed to stitch the instructions move forward, towards the corners.

1.

It is necessary to alter the seam allowance by yourself. In this seam allowance, if you encounter an angle, you will need to secure the needle in the fabric. Side by side , you must lift your presser foot.

2. The fabric will be hung on the left side, and the needle that is lowered will help ensure that the fabric stays in place.

3. Adjust the presser foot of the machine to allow you to continue sewing using the altered fabric and sewing machine.

The Rounding Curves

You'll need to curve corners to round them in the method we discussed earlier within the section on corner. When you are attempting to circle those corners, you can make only the tilted hand movements which will enable you to perform the adjusted movements. If you want to round corners that are more tilted, you'll need move your cloth then move the needle along.

When your fabric becomes difficult to control, go at a steady pace and check if the fabric is being adjusted. If not, you can lower your needle and then raise the presser foot in tandem. You might have to repeat this motion several times until the fabric adjusts to your needs.

If you have curves in seams, we suggest to cut the seam allowances from different spots so that your dress will be simple to flip to the right side. However, one thing you must be careful is to cut the snips with care. When you are cutting the edges, you could make a cut in your seam. Make sure you snip the seam carefully and with care.

Making buttonholes

The majority of clothes are worn by people come with at least one closure that help them work well and fit also. There are buttons as a type of closure is possible to incorporate to your clothes. Making button holes doesn't seem easy and isn't always easy when you aren't familiar with the procedure thoroughly. The good thing is that a lot of the newer machines come with connected buttons with automatic functionality which can simplify the process for you.

You must be extremely cautious to ensure the results are flawless. Sometimes it can be difficult to put all buttonholes on the same straight line in which they should, however paying attention to the details will make a huge difference.

There are a variety of kinds of buttonholes and the one you choose in your design will depend on the type of fabric you're using as well as the buttons, too. For instance, the square buttons are utilized on heavy to medium fabrics. The keyhole buttonholethat is similar to the keyhole, can be found on medium to heavy-weight fabrics and is compatible with more thick or larger buttons. If you're using a medium to fine heavy fabric could make use of the round buttons that are attached to the round-end buttonhole.

This is how to make buttonholes by using the buttonhole feature that automatically comes on your machine:

Note the location where buttons on your garment will appear with your tailor's chalk.

Make sure you set your machine at the correct setting based on the type of buttonhole you'd like to create.

Attach the buttonhole foot in order to get to go.

The dimension of the button, to establish the dimensions of the button hole. This can be accomplished through placing the buttons inside the button holder towards the bottom of the foot, and then pressing the button holder closely over the button.

- Now , pull the lever of the buttonhole to the maximum extent you can.

Place your fabric on the buttonhole foot, then move the needle upwards and downwards several times.

Begin sewing the buttonhole. There is no need to do anything as the sewing will happen automatically. Start by sewing the row to left firstand then next row.

Zipper installation

This is a different kind or closure every tailor has to know about so that you are able to create garments that are comfortable and good in appearance. The process of installing a zipper can be quite complicated and can be a bit intimidating for the first timer, but after a few attempts, you'll succeed. When it comes to zippers, you need to practice to be able to do it correctly every time you complete a fantastic project. It is important to make sure that you are able to install your zippers as if you were a professional each time, so take a few tries and learn the technique.

There are a variety of methods which can be employed in the case of installing the zipper. This includes slots seam zipper insertion as well as lapper zipper insertion zippers on lined and face garments and invisible zipper insertions, among numerous others. There are various methods for covering the zipper's edge that you must be aware of to make sure that your work is always tidy.

Sewing pleats and darts

Darts are the elements that are included in clothing to ensure they are in a perfect shape that is able to follow the body. It is important to know how to draw, how to sew, and then press to create the ideal dart. Pleats are also helpful in sewing because it works to give your project the perfect shape. Pleats increase the texture, and understanding how to make pleats can make something unique and captivating to any style.

Making pleats and darts correctly takes time and practice can help you master the art. Precision is always called for as a single mistake can ruin your entire outfit. There are many methods of measuring darts and using an tracing sheet and a trace wheel is an ideal choice for someone who is just starting out. Then, you can use custom-made chalk for marking the start and ending of your dart legs.

Here are some typical types of darts you'll need to be aware of:

Bust darts

- French darts

- Contour darts

- Waist darts

Topstitching

This is basically any type of stitching that is applied to the top of the fabric. It is a crucial technique to use when one is sewing or tailoring, since it is designed to add a decorative element of the garment and also performing other essential functions. The new tailor will be intimidated by topstitching, particularly since it must look stylish and attractive. Because the stitching will be visible in the correct side of the fabric, the stitching is required to be done perfectly and that's why it is important to learn the proper techniques before you can apply the technique for your projects.

The process of topstitching does not need to be as daunting as it may sound. All you require is an appropriate thread with the fabric in order to start. If you don't have an exact match, you may select a thread that is blending perfectly to the material. In the event that there are errors and blunders, they'll be hard to spot. Another thing that works out for you is lots of repetition. Make sure to sew slowly until you're able to create an ideal top stitch. Be aware that you could always make use of an edge ripper in the event there is a mistake, so don't panic even if you didn't get it perfect on your first go.

Chapter 17: The Special Techniques For Sewing

In the final section, we've made an effort to ensure that all beginners they are able to grasp the fundamentals of seaming and stitching. However, for the beginner it isn't enough. You must continue to work in order to learn the specific methods of stitching and sewing.

Hemming

Hemming is essential at the bottom of pants, at the necklines and at the bottom of sleeves. Additionally, the fabric's raveling is prevented by creating stunning Hemming. The following are the main stages of hemming

1. Then turn the fabric around in a manner that allows for a proper seam allowance. In the majority of cases, an inch turn will suffice. Once you've completed the turn, you must press the fabric on the entire turn. It gives the fabric a smooth and pressed appearance.

2. Pin the folded area so that the fabric is able to settle within your hands. Additionally, if you use too many pins they will ultimately disturb your sewing, therefore you must adjust your sewing precisely in this respect. Sew the press folds.

3.

There are instances when you require soft the hems. In these situations you'll need to make your hem with your hands using a needle as well as the thread.

Utilize two threads to form an assembly

Gathering is a technique for sewing that is mainly used for the various dresses and accessories that require a little of a ruffle. It gives amazing fullness to the skirt, sleeves, and caps. The gathering technique implemented requires additional fabric, and it is imperative that if you plan to gather for the event, you plan ahead in order to be prepared with all the required materials and items before the time. Gatherings can be very or intensive and in both instances the amount of fabric needed will differ.

When gathering techniques, the initial stage is to establish an accurate seam allowance. The most common thing people do not consider is that there should be a two seam allowance. Because there will be two seams for gathering thus, you must ensure that your seam allowance is double over the standard.

Another method used for gathering process is known as basting. In order to do that, you be sure to keep your stitch length the longest length you can get.

Then, you will make the first seam on all the way around the fabric with the width of 1/4 inch. When you're done with the first seam, you can make another seam, this time at an interval of 1/4 inch. This will result in two seams in succession. Be careful not to cut the threads off at the ends at the end of every seam. The threads are used to make the gathers.

Once you're done with seams remove the threads from one endwhile holding your hand on the other. A gentle pull will allow the gathering to take place. Adjust the gathering order that the gathers are placed equally across the fabric.

Another method is pulling the threads off both ends to create more filled threads.

Applique work

This is a stunning method of pattern-making, that can enhance the look of your outfit or other accessory.

1.

The shape and size of the fabric can be cut into various patterns. These are the patterns that appear as patterns on a different cloth. Therefore, cut the shape precisely.

2.

Then, you'll put the cut piece onto the fabric, and then you'll need to apply an ideal shape. The market is brimming with items that will help in enhancing the capacity for the piece you cut to be a stickers onto the fabric. One of these products is fusible web.

3. Utilize a zigzag stitch in order to hold it in place and cut the pattern in the spot. stitch along the corners, and around the edges so that the pattern doesn't become distorted. A trick to do this is to make sure that the zigzag stitch stays only on the area that you have put in the fabric. Don't stitch the underside fabric to the top.

French seam

French seams are another stunning design option to make your dress look extremely attractive and fashionable. French seams prevent any form of raveling of the fabric. You can effectively stop raveling with simply utilizing the simple technique of French seams.

1.

The first step is to turn your fabric on its wrong side, and then stitch it up to the point at which you want it to end.

2. Turn it over to the left side and stitch until you reach the edge to the material. Be sure this seam lies separated from the previous seam and it takes advantage of the gap left.

These are only a few examples of the techniques used in sewing that are commonly used in diverse sewing styles. While these are provided in a step-by-step method, you can create your own unique techniques using the hit and try method.

Flat-felled seams

They are often found on men's clothes. They are used to give an clean and professional appearance to the finished product whenever you're sewing garments, sportswear, as well as other clothes. This is a durable seam, which is why it's durable. it will give your clothing more structure , without having to increase the bulk of the clothing.

This is how it's completed - one end is folded over the other raw edge Then it is finished by stitching it flat.

This type of seam is perfect for reversed garments which are designed to look identical from both angles. If you're making a garment that has narrow curves, you should not sew these seams.

Bias bound seams

Bias seams are also known as"the Hong Kong seam finish. They're basically a method to add an amount of knowledge to the garment you are making. This is a fantastic way to inject some color into the insides of your garments so that they appear more attractive.

The raw edge of the fabric is enclosed completely by the bias tape. This gives an clean appearance on the inside of the fabric.

This seam is not straightforward, but mastering it is a great skill to master since you are able to include something gorgeous to your work to make them more attractive. This method is best applied to heavy clothing or ones that don't have an lined.

Making use of a rotary cutting machine

Every tailor should have an rotary cutter as well as cutting mat. But, you must be able to cut with a rotary cutting machine in order to utilize the tools of a lifetime effectively. A rotary cutter will allow you to cut patterns with ease as well as faster and more precisely. The cutting mat can assist you in protecting the surface of your work from cuts that aren't needed.

The rotary cutter must be kept in tip-top shape, which is why you may need to keep an inventory of rotary blades to be able to modify them to your preferences for sharpness.

Princess seams

They are basically a form of darts which are utilized to create rounded curves that shape women's clothes. What you can achieve with princess seams is a rounded, slimmer appearance that must be customized to the wearer's mind. These seams are perfect for fitting jackets and dresses for bringing out an elongated, sculpted and slender waist. They are often found in wedding gowns as well as couture gowns however they are gradually gaining popularity in the majority of dresses for women.

There are numerous other decorative seams offered in the majority of modern sewing machines you can make use of to get the best out of each task you tackle.

Pressing and ironing

Ironing is an essential component of sewing since it assists in removing wrinkles from a garment you're working on. Ironing is distinct from pressing, though both require an iron, however pressing is the most recommended method when sewing. The process of ironing, which involves moving the iron around the fabric, could be detrimental to the garment that's why pressing is recommended when sewing clothes. Pressing is the process of placing the iron onto the fabric and letting it stay there for a couple of seconds before taking it off. Pressing won't alter fibres in your clothing or fabric, and will aid in setting and blend your stitches , allowing you to have a smooth crisp seam. You must take the proper care of your garment or fabric while pressing it constantly.

Curves and corners are clipped.

This is a simple but crucial method which can be very helpful when sewing. Making seams that have curvatures and corners isn't an easy job and, on these projects you will have to work for your life to ensure that the garment stays on its feet at all times. Cutting corners and curves could make the job easier for you.

Cutting a corner on a diagonal, near the seam but not too close , will provide you with a beautiful and simple corner to work with and it will look great when you flip your work upside down.

The same is true with curves, too. Curves that resemble mountains are able to be notched, and those that resemble valleys could be clipped for convenience and a perfect finishing.

Stitching your stay

This technique can prevent any distortion to your curves. Stay stitching is carried out in a curve. It is done by setting your stich length to about 1.5 and then beginning your stitching 1/8 inch away from the stitching line.

Curves must be stitched after cutting to prevent distortion, as shifting your fabric just several times following cutting can cause a cause a mess in the curve.

Fussy cutting

This is a method can be applied to an embroidered fabric you wish to work with to create a distinct motif. This is a simpler method to make designs that can be added to projects or garments intended to be used for decorating your home.

To get to get the best cuts, make a cut around the design you are trying to eliminate and ensure that plenty of room is left. Cut the motif down to the actual size, leaving a tiny seam allowance. Then, you can put the design on the fabric . To keep it in place you can stitch satin stitches or apply spray adhesive.

Bar tracks can be used to track bar patrons.

Bar tracks can be used to strengthen areas that will be subject to lots of pressure once the work is completed. This includes, for example, pockets openings. If they are not reinforced they will become weaker with time and could cause damage to the fabric. The bar tracks are made by sewing with your machine using an zigzag stitch. Alternatively, you can sew it manually using whip stich.

Chapter 18: Sewing Tutorials- Simple To Follow

In this chapter, you will find the basics of sewing, there are tutorials that serve as the primary guide for those who wish to practice sewing at home.

A button that you sew on:

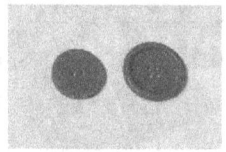

The reason to explain button sewing is because of its regular necessity in every household routine. Sometimes, just hanging a button requires assistance from someone else, so this is the time to help our readers familiar with this easy task. Understanding the basics first is much more important than getting into the tougher ones.

On the market there are two kinds of buttons.

Flat buttons comprise an entire body as a whole, to where threads are managed directly to connect the button.

Shank buttons differ from other buttons in that they have a small eyelet-like opening that is then extended towards on the reverse of the button. The back of the button opens into an opening that serves as a way of connecting the button. These holes extend beyond the back of the button, and are drilled to attach the button. Shank buttons are generally employed for purpose of decoration, since the top of shank buttons is able to fulfill the purpose of ornamentation.

Sewing:

1. Cut a thread approximately 24" length.

2. Thread into the needle, and then create an elongated loop in such a way that it is folded in on itself.

1.

By catching each end of your thread tie an untie at the end to be working with double thread. This will strengthen the button. Make sure you trim the thread

2.

Place a marker on the fabric that you would like to put the button. By marking the area, you can pull the needle upwards.

3. Create a stitch in the form of an "X" on the spot you are at.

4.

By stitching the "X" while you steer your needle, insert it into one of the holes at the point that the button is slightly higher than the surface of the fabric. The stitch should be diagonally across the fabric until all four holes are completely stitched. Sometimes you might receive a button with two holes. In this case, stitching is based on only two holes.

5. Then, move your needle and thread from side-to-side along the fabric However, this time, the thread will be just under the button.

6. The thread should be wrapped tightly around the bottom of the button. If you doubt that it is light, wrap it three or four times. Make a loop , and cut the thread.

If you want to stitch a shank button the fundamental steps are identical, and only a few minor adjustments will be required. Since there is an already-shank, it is not necessary to create any space between the button and the fabric. Furthermore, while sewing through holes you'll only stitch the shank since the shank functions for the purpose of the holes. Therefore, you won't stitch over and over just like you would in the case of flat buttons.

Pockets stitched

If you're interested in sewing, you'll find the majority of two kinds of pockets.

1. Side seam Pocket 2. Pocket on Shirt

sewing Side Seam Pockets Side Seam Pocket

1. The extensions can be placed to the sides of your skirt or frock. Extensions are used as the fronts for the pockets. The size should be around 2"more then the hands in the pocket.

2.

Draw the pockets into the desired form.

3. Mark using a pencil. Stitch on both sides of those corners on the faces. Cut the edge away and the stitching should not cut. Create a stitching area along the edge so that the thread can increase its durability.

4.

Then stitch the pocket in a manner to ensure that it's stitched to the opposite side of the shirt or skirt. Stitching should be done on the edges that curve.

5. You will then stitch the skirt or the shirt onto which you will place the pocket. Put the stitches on towards the back of the

skirt back side seam. When sewing this seam, be sure to not sew the pocket's edge. edges will be sewn to the seam. Press the pocket firmly to give it a neat appearance.

Sewing the shirt's Pocket

1. Cut the pocket into the shape of a rectangle. The size of the pocket you desire should be marked, and the allowance should be for 1/2" for the upper hem and seam allowances on all three sides.

2. Press the lower edges three times using an iron. Also , press the hem under.

3. Flip the pocket over to its right. Create an Topstitch the upper hem in place

4.

The pocket is placed in the dress or shirt front. Make sure the pocket is facing up.

5. The shirt should be stitched around the three lower sides. On the fourth, which is the one that will be the top and is open.

Make sure the corners are strengthened of the pocket of your shirt by stitching.

Simple home decor

It's easy to start with a simple decorating plan for your home. Here's an example of an Easter egg-themed decorating your home. It is necessary to have a flowered fabric to complete this idea.

What you require:

Pinking shears or pinking cutting rotary cutter

* Assorted pastel fabrics

*12" Square cardstock

* An egg template

Method:

1. Cut 1 1/2x13" strips from the various fabrics. Cut as many strips as you can in order to be able to do more.

Make use of your pinking scissors or a pinking rotary cutter reduce one edge of each strip to create the look of wavy and sophisticated.

* Place one strip of fabric over the 12"-square sheet of paper, so that the edges that are pink are covered by the bottom of the sheet. Sew across the straight edge of your machine. Make sure to stitch all of the fabric strips until the cardstock has been covered with fabric strips.

Flip the paper over , and using your egg template trace the egg onto the paper. Try to place as many eggs onto the paper as you possibly can.

* Sew both sides of the lines of each egg to keep the fabric strips in place.

* Finally, cut out eggs along the lines you have drawn. Be sure to not cutting through the stitches.

A heart pincushion

A heart-shaped pincushion is simple to create and the end result are amazing. It is possible to create your own pincushion to hold your pins when you work on an important task.

Materials required:

* Heart template

Two squares each of print pink fabric

* 1 square lightweight fusible web

* Pencil

One square of pink craft felt

* Polyester fiberfill

Method

* Create your heart applique with your fusible web. Lay on the fabric, paper facing up over the heart design and then use a pencil to draw the heart shape. The pattern should be pressed onto the pink craft felt as directed. Allow it to cool and then cut the pattern using the lines of the market.

Take off the paper on the bottom of the heart and put it in the square of pink. Be sure to fuse the applique to the square. Let it cool.

* By using a contrast color thread, stitch onto the heart with blanket stitches with

the sewing device. The white color of thread would be a great option.

Make sure you have the pincushion assemble and then sew by hand using a similar color of thread over the areas that are not closed for closure of the pincushion.

Holders for tissues

They will be not just fun to make, but also very useful when they're done.

Materials required:

* 2 rectangles of matching fabric to cover on the back of the tray holder

One rectangle to use for the back

* Sharpie marker

Crafts felt white and black

* Tailor's chalk

* Embroidery thread: white and black

* Pieces of the pattern

Method:

* Put the tissue cover together.

* Join the pieces along the edges.

* Sew the rectangle parts together while leaving a margin for seams.

* Create some patterns that you like.

* Turn it upside down to make it a complete tissue holder.

Installing a zipper that is basic

Zippers are terrifying, and they are , but did you realize that it is possible to put a zipper in place without having to think about it as much? Here's a simple follow guideline;

You'll need an zipper foot in order to get going. The zipper foot is small with a notch along the left side to accommodate the needle, and one to the side as well. This helps the presser foot be placed right next to the zipper, so that the seam is in close proximity to the zipper that you are making.

Take the fabric pieces you'd like to zip up, along with your zipper.

Join the fabric pieces. Then, flip them over to the opposite side, and then press the edges of both pieces open and flat. This will give you your starting point as well as the ending line of the zipper.

Place the middle of the zipper's teeth with the middle of the open seam, and then secure the zipper together with pins or tape, depending on the method you prefer to utilize. Make sure that the zipper is held to the middle of your seam.

Flip the fabric over and mark where the zipper will end to ensure that you don't stitch on the metal piece that is at the bottom of the zip. It is possible to put a pin on that location.

Set your needle to begin sewing along the bottom which will form the seam. With the right side facing up put your fabric on the presser foot , and then slide it up until you reach the mark. Make sure that the distance between tooth to point which you're sewing is the same throughout. Back stitch several times in the beginning and before continuing sewing until the close. Backstitch after the last.

Change your needle alignment to the left side, so that you can stitch the opposite side, as well. Make sure that the distance you maintained on the other side is the that you maintain on this side as well to ensure uniformity.

After that after that, you can confirm that the zipper is in good working order.

Chapter 19: Making Sewing Patterns For Beginners

Sewing patterns is a ability that novices should learn , particularly if you're thinking of designing your own clothing. For beginners, it is not necessary to purchase sewing patterns in basis of which they can begin making their own clothing, however it is best method to start to learn the different ways to use patterns before you begin creating your own designs. If this appeals to you, start by purchasing one or two patternsand then begin to practice with them. You'll learn a lot when you're finished, and will be able to work with patterns as a professional.

The best sewing patterns to begin with

When you are purchasing the sewing pattern for your initial project It is best to opt for patterns that are simple and simple. The last thing you want to learn is complicated techniques that will make learning difficult. There are patterns that are clearly marked as simple and quick and they are the ideal ones to begin with. Begin working on clothes which only require a couple of pieces that you are able to join together. This will not only make the process simple for you but will it will also inspire you to keep to the next level. This will guarantee that your first venture will be a success.

Pick your fabric well. It is important to choose the right fabric for beginning sewers. Avoid slippery and stretchy fabrics, for instance, as they will give you a difficult time setting up and sew on them. A better option for beginners is an unwoven textile made of cotton that's simple to sew and set.

The first time you buy sewing patterns, it's the perfect time to purchase your own.

Nowadays is the best method to purchase sewing patterns is to shop on the internet. The internet makes the process much easier, and allows you to easily define the type of pattern you want when you search for year. If you are just beginning sewing, you'll need pick the pattern that is simple in modifications and complications, to ensure that you know how to create the perfect shape of your piece just prior to making ornaments.

There are certain aspects to take into account when you are choosing sewing patterns. the most important are:

I) Make sure you pick something you are happy with and which you think you would be comfortable wearing. It is not necessary to waste time with patterns or creating something you don't intend to put to an effective way. Remember that the first person who will be able to appreciate your work is you therefore resist the urge to make an impression on someone else in the beginning.

II) Be sure to purchase patterns that clearly labeled for novices. Certain brands will clearly label these patterns as simple and quick while others simply label them for those who are just beginning. Make certain you're choosing an easy pattern that you could quickly master.

II) At this point you will have an understanding of the basic terms you can reference when you're getting ready to sew. That means that if you get an item that has terms that you don't understand it is best to stay clear of this pattern. You must be aware of what the pattern intends to accomplish. In this is how you will begin to tackle an assignment that you're capable of handling.

Iv) Read the reviews too. Beginning users will always give opinions on patterns they've attempted. You should find out what they thought of the patterns prior to deciding to purchase it. It will affect your decision and can affect your purchase in a significant way. It is unlikely that you will purchase patterns that are difficult for someone who is new to the craft because there is no guarantee it will be simple for you. If you can, pick one that has been adored by a lot of people who have tried it, and you could find yourself enjoying making it.

Selecting the correct size

If you are creating your first project for you, it is important to select the appropriate size of pattern so that it is sized correctly. The majority of sewing brands that are available today have various sizes of the exact pattern, making it extremely easy to find the right size for the pattern you want.

You must have your measurements measured first to be able to make use of them to select the patterns you want to create. Many people be tempted to use sizes that are ready to wear to make this choice. It is important to understand that sizes for ready-to-wear differ greatly from sizes used in sewing patterns. This is because each body is different. If a particular clothing fits you perfectly isn't a guarantee that it's the perfect fit. If you're making your own clothes it is important to aim at perfection above all else. It is essential to determine the exact measurements you need to make sure that the clothes you'll be sewing will fit comfortably.

There's a broad range of figures to pick from when you purchase the sewing patterns you need:

Misses' patterns they are designed intended for a well-developed, well-proportioned figure, which is approximately 5'6" tall.

* Women's designs - these are designed for a bigger figure, which is around 5'6" tall

* Designs for girls', boys', kids', baby and toddlers'

* Girls' Plus patternsfor older girls

* Patterns for men

It is important to know that you are able to alter the length or the length of the garment quickly to enhance the fit since the majority of patterns won't fit perfectly. Keep in mind that just like recipes in cookbooks the pattern is intended to serve as a reference but does not have to be followed strictly in the event that the result might not exactly match what you're hoping to accomplish. The good thing is that certain patterns made by specific brands will include clear guidelines for how to enhance the fit, because they are aware that some of these sizes won't be suitable for certain people, even if they belong to the categorical categories.

One thing tailors should be aware of when creating their own clothing is that they are able to modify the patterns to be able to tailor them in the exact way they would like. As you progress in your capabilities, you'll be able to combine sizes to make an amazing design for yourself. If you are worried that you'll face some issues in this regard, you could begin by learning the basics of pattern modification at first, and you'll have a much easier time doing it afterward.

Instructions and pattern markings

Every sewing pattern comes with instructions and markings. This could be difficult for a novice tailor as they've never had anything like it before. The key to comprehending the markings and directions is taking the time to go through them thoroughly. Don't be in a rush to begin sewing them together as you could make a mistake and ruin the whole pattern. Some patterns include explanations and symbols as well. They will aid you in understanding the whole thing, and then you can begin making your own garment.

Chapter 20: Sewing Tips To Help Begin

Sewing is fun and you'll surely enjoy sewing. Beginning is the most difficult part, as the majority of beginners don't realize they can do it until they begin. It is among the most rewarding abilities you'll learn throughout your lifetime, and with some tips that you follow, you can ensure that you'll have fewer problems along the way.

1.) Cut seam allowances for seams enclosed. The large seam allowances in handmade patterns can be very bulky on cuffs, facings as well as waistbands, collars, and plackets. It is important to reduce the seam allowances to cut down on time while cutting, trimming, grading as well as notching following sewing. This will ensure that your seams look clean after sewing. If you are beginners this method that will make the process easier to follow before you can master greater seam allowances. Keep in mind that bigger seam allowances are typically designed to allow you some space in the event of mistakes. If you make the right choice from the beginning then you won't have the issue.

2.) Make sure to cut your piece and make a mark in one go to prevent confusion. After you have cut the pieces you'll require then tie them up and then place them into bags. This will make sure that you're working quickly throughout the day. As you place them in the bag ensure that you've arranged them in an order such that you are aware of which to look for and at what time.

3.) Cut clean. Learn to cut properly before making important decisions to ensure that you are skilled when cutting. When you have clear cuts, half of the work is done. Use a large table to make sure that you're cutting with precision every time. Purchase a rotary cutter, too to cut better than cutting tools. Purchase a rotary mat to the table to prevent messing the work surface.

4.) For marking your notches, don't need to cut diamonds that can be difficult and frustrating , particularly in the beginning stages of mastering the art of. It is always possible to use the nips as they are more precise and will not be easily frayed for a clean finish, or worse, make your seams more brittle.

5.) You don't have to secure your designs onto the cloth. They can be held to the fabric with weights. This can save time and energy. Additionally, if you work with a material that is delicate, you'll be able to protect it from harm that could result from pins and holes.

6.) Reduce time spent by focusing on the smaller parts first, and then joining the pieces to form the final garment. Make sure that you work on all tasks that are related in parallel and then proceed by sewing. If you follow this step by process, you'll feel a sense of accomplishment when you complete the whole garment.

7.) Cut your designs along the cut line. This will result in clean patterns all the time and you won't have to spend a lot of time making them perfect. After cutting the pieces, make sure you press them thoroughly. This way, you'll ensure that there aren't any mistakes on the fabric before beginning the actual sewing.

8.) Do the buttonholes first. Then, make use of them to show you on where buttons are needed. When it comes to buttonholes, you should don't use a seam-ripper which can consume the longest time. Use a punch instead, and see how speedy it will be.

9) Avoid pinning if you can. Pins can slow down tailoring, and if you're looking to finish your project in time, you may have cut out that part. Pins can cause distortion to your seams also, and pins may cause damage to the needles. It is possible to use both hands when sewing, so that you don't have to utilize pins. Find the perfect corners from start to finish and make sure that your edges of the raw material match too and then you can begin sewing.

10) You can save a lot of energy and time by sewing in a continuous fashion. It is not necessary sewing one item of fabric after another, you can sew them in a continuous fashion and then separate them once you are on the press board.

11.) 11) Sew additional seams in the beginning then press all of them later. There is no need to go between the machine and the press board, which can be exhausting and time-consuming.

12) Create a press station for yourself rather than relying on an ironing table. It may not be good enough and could take a long time to complete particularly if you're working on a bulky garment. When you've got the room, construct an efficient press station. This will allow for you to design a plan of the various pieces you're working on, to allow you to press them as needed and achieve great results. This will help make it easier to move between stations within your workspace.

Chapter 21: Advanced Sewing Techniques You Should Be Educated

As you become proficient at sewing it is likely that you will need to improve your abilities at one point or the other so you can accomplish something more on you sewing device. There will never be a time when you're an absolute beginner, but you'll eventually be an expert tailor . this is just a few of the methods you need to master so that you can demonstrate your skills and make projects that will be appreciated and used by a lot of people:

Traditional tailoring

It may appear odd considering that this is a discussion of the most advanced methods, but remember that you must start somewhere. A few years ago, all the latest sewing techniques weren't available and traditional methods were sufficient to create a garment that could be used for a long period of period of time. This is the best first step and you can increase your knowledge as you sew more clothing. Traditional tailoring hasn't been able to lose its importance in contemporary times. It is very well thought-of and some tailors continue to employ certain old methods when creating their garments to create something useful at the end of the day.

By adding pockets for welts

Welt pockets are popular on many of the best coats and jackets that you can purchase in the present. They can also be found on purses, trousers as well as skirts in addition to other clothes. This is an essential method that adds the most worth to your projects. Expert tailors will not be able to complete a project without welt pockets since this is a fantastic idea to test out each time. There are various kinds of welt pockets that can incorporate into a garment. There are one-welt pocket, double welt pockets the ones equipped with zippers, flaps and many other. The principle technique used in creating the welt pockets is easy to master, after which it is possible to add some flair depending on the type of garment you're working with and the fabric you're working with.

Trims and pipe

Trims and pipes don't need to be present in your design, but their presence can make a big impact on the final outcome. They can make a significant difference to the final product. Piped seams for instance , or edges provide a great worth to a pattern's lines. They also can provide color to the clothing and make it appear more appealing than it would in the absence of seams piped. The piping is readily available however certain tailors prefer making their own piping with a the piping foot, or even zippers. This method can be applied with a waistband for a skirt.

Trim , on the other hand is a great way to highlight one color on a fabric printed, or even on an boucle material. Trims can be made in the hands of a professional tailor, or you can make them with the sewing machines. Consider trimming the collarline on a coat in your next project and master the art of trimming.

Complex designs

Simple methods and techniques are always easy to master, and they are mastered in just some days. The problem with easy techniques is that everybody else is already trying them out so you won't have the opportunity to stand out from the other tailors. The more intricate designs may take time, but they are the reason behind the incredible designs that are seen on the market every day.

Therefore, you must learn certain complex structures so that you are able to develop great designs you'll be happy trying out. Complex constructions can be very beneficial and will assure that the tailor pays particular attention to each and every detail. They increase your precision and increase your imagination and allow you to create pictures that are captivating and distinctive. Test everything that pops into your mind , and then add some skills you acquire every day, and discover how amazing it will look at the final.

Underlining

Underlining is made based on the fabric is used. There are other reasons you might want to apply an underlining to your clothes. If you're working with silk, which is light in weight for instance you could apply underlining to improve the fabric's strength and reduce wrinkles that the fabric may develop. Underlining can be utilized on woolen clothes also for the purpose of doing rid of facings.

Underlining is used to make the fabric's exterior stand out particularly if it is an outstanding design. The technique of underlining will teach you an entirely new technique, that is stitching by hand inside the fabric. This can be useful when you begin to tackle large-scale projects.

Conclusion

At the close in the text, I would like to let my readers feel happy at the fact that they have a helpful book that will not only help them bring their talents out however, it can also improve their skills of sewing more refined and sophisticated. I am convinced that we've achieved our goal of making our readers completely informed about the basic process of learning to sew. One thing I'd like to highlight at the final section is the necessity to continue practicing. We've covered all techniques using a step by method approach however, what we want from readers is that they utilize this information to the maximum.

We've followed an approach that is step-by-step to help those who are new to sewing get an easy and efficient sewing lessons. The basic tools and devices are included so that readers can pick the right tool for the various types of fabric and design. We hope that our readers become proficient in all of their sewing endeavors.

Best of luck and have fun sewing! !

www.ingramcontent.com/pod-product-compliance
Lightning Source LLC
Chambersburg PA
CBHW070100120526
44589CB00033B/1048